THE **FLOORING HANDBOOK**

W9-BGY-620

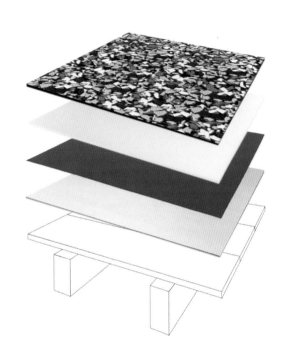

THE **FLOORING HANDBOOK**

The complete guide to choosing and installing floors

DENNIS JEFFRIES

FIREFLY BOOKS

A Firefly Book

Published by Firefly Books Ltd. 2004

Copyright © 2004 Quarto Publishing Inc.

All rights reserved. No part of this publication may be reproduced, stored in a retrieval system, or transmitted in any form or by any means, electronic, mechanical, photocopying, recording or otherwise, without the prior written permission of the Publisher.

First printing

Publisher Cataloging-in-Publication Data (U.S.)

Jeffries, Dennis, 1930–

The flooring handbook : the complete guide to choosing and installing floors / Dennis Jeffries. —1st ed.
[144] p. : col. photos. ; cm.
Includes index.
Summary: Guide to every type of home flooring for both the beginner and more experienced installer. Flooring types covered include tiles, stone, wood, laminate, vinyl, cork, rubber and leather.
ISBN 1-55297-753-6
ISBN 1-55297-752-8 (pbk.)
1. Flooring.   2. Floor coverings.   3. Floors—Amateurs' manuals.   I. Title.
698.9 22   TH2525.J44   2004

National Library of Canada Cataloguing in Publication

Jeffries, Dennis, 1930–
The flooring handbook : the complete guide to choosing and installing floors / Dennis Jeffries.
Includes index.
ISBN 1-55297-753-6 (bound.)
ISBN 1-55297-752-8 (pbk.)
1. Flooring--Handbooks, manuals, etc. I. Title.
TH2525.J43 2004   690'.16 C2003-906682-7

Published in the United States in 2004 by
Firefly Books (U.S.) Inc.
P.O. Box 1338, Ellicott Station
Buffalo, New York 14205

Published in Canada in 2004 by
Firefly Books Ltd.
3680 Victoria Park Avenue
Toronto, Ontario, M2H 3K1

Printed in China

QUAR.FLOO

WARNING AND DISCLAIMER: The author and publisher have made every effort to ensure that all instructions contained within this book are accurate and safe, and cannot accept liability for any resulting injury, damage or loss to persons or property however it may arise. If in any doubt as to the correct or safe procedure to follow for any home improvement task, seek professional advice.

CONTENTS

GETTING STARTED

You may already have in mind the "look" you want for your home, but don't rush out to buy a new floor straightaway. The key to installing a floor yourself is thorough preparation. This section will help you assess your site and choose a flooring that suits the location—as well as your tastes, budget and level of expertise. For inspiration, and more information about your chosen floor, turn to the relevant flooring section later in the book. There are hundreds of photographs of fabulous floors, grouped into "hard," "resilient," "wood" and "soft," to enable you to compare similar options. Find out more about durability, maintenance and design possibilities, and check out the skills required by looking at the step-by-step installation instructions. Then return to this section for essential information about preparing the site: leveling the subfloor, waterproofing, trimming doors, planning the layout and much more.

1.1

Choosing the right floor

USEFUL TIP
Always check your local building code before beginning work: you may require a permit.

Today's homeowner is faced with such an extensive range of flooring choices that selecting the right floor can almost be harder than actually installing it! Flooring is one of the most important features of a room, dictating its style, atmosphere and, often, even how the room will be used. It is important to choose carefully, especially since installing a new floor can require considerable investment in time and money. When you are deciding whether you want carpet or laminate, terra-cotta or stainless steel, vinyl or rubber, you should think of more than the floor's appearance. Can you afford to install and maintain the floor? Do you have the required expertise to lay it or should you hire a professional? Will the floor withstand the wear and tear associated with the normal use of the room? Are you after comfort or style, or most concerned that the flooring should be environmentally friendly? Whatever your primary concerns, the following pages provide guidelines on what to consider before making your choice.

Floors can be split into four distinct groups: hard, resilient, wood and soft. Each group shares certain characteristics and methods of installation.

HARD FLOORS are usually laid in tile form with adhesive or mortar, and include ceramic, stone and brick. They are often spectacular and durable, but also cold and expensive. Metal, marble, granite, glass and terrazzo floors are particularly distinctive and contemporary, but they are also much more difficult to install than other hard floors, and should only be laid by professionals.

RESILIENT FLOORS are comfortable underfoot, easy to install and clean, and offer resistance to denting. Floors such as vinyl, linoleum and cork are cost-effective, but leather is very expensive. These are the brightest of floors, with a huge range of colors and patterns available. They are also the thinnest type of covering, which means that the subfloor must be especially level.

WOOD FLOORS remain one of the most popular flooring choices. This group includes laminate flooring, which may feature a hard-floor simulation but is laid in a similar way to a floating wood floor. Floating floors can easily be tackled by the amateur (and the subfloor does not need to be perfectly level), but you must always remember to protect wood from moisture. Gluing and nailing wood, however, are much more difficult methods.

SOFT FLOORS comprise carpet and natural-fiber coverings. They produce a warm, comfortable environment, but can be difficult to install and clean, and must be laid with other fittings such as tackless strips and padding. Padding will absorb slight unevenness in the subfloor, so leveling before installation is not critical.

FLOORS FOR YOUR HOME

The varying characteristics of floors make them suited to different areas of a house.

LOCATION	MOST POPULAR	LESS SUITABLE	NOT SUITABLE
Entrance hall Flooring in this location should be welcoming and able to cope with heavy traffic, which may be wet and dirty. Any durable flooring can be used for a hallway, and the choice is largely directed by interior decoration.	Carpet, wood, laminate, natural-fiber coverings and any of the hard floors. Mosaic or terrazzo, for example, might be overwhelming in a large space, but can be very effective in a hall.	Vinyl has a synthetic feel that is not always welcoming. Cheap linoleum may be too informal for use in an entrance hall.	Floors such as cork and leather are not durable enough for such high-traffic areas.
Kitchen and utility areas The floor must be easy to clean and suitable for a high level of traffic. Comfort and warmth underfoot may also be considerations.	Linoleum and vinyl are simple to clean, and these floors can be easily and cheaply updated as styles change. Terra-cotta, slate, ceramic or even mosaic can give a rustic or sophisticated look. All are very durable, but cold (terra-cotta is the warmest) and unforgiving to dropped dishes or glasses.	Cork is warm underfoot and easy to clean, but may be too soft for a kitchen floor. Wood and laminate are often used, but must be protected from moisture.	Carpet and natural-fiber floors may be comfortable, but they trap dirt and are very difficult to clean.

LOCATION	MOST POPULAR	LESS SUITABLE	NOT SUITABLE
Formal rooms When it comes to living rooms, dining rooms, studies and libraries, the flooring is largely determined by the way the room is used, and what style is preferred. In living rooms, particularly more formal ones, practical issues matter least—effect counts for most. Cost, however, is one issue that you will have to consider, especially if the area is large.	For years, carpet has been the obvious choice for comfort, value for money and range of color. Wood is also very suitable and is supplied in many styles, from contemporary, grain-free pale maple to rustic oak. Hard floors look spectacular, but unless you live in a year-round hot climate, they are more suitable for formal dining rooms than living rooms.	Leather is a luxurious option for a low-traffic study or library, but it is expensive. A top-end linoleum design or high-tech rubber floor could make a strong contribution to a contemporary living room, but this look is not for everyone.	Standard grades of linoleum, vinyl and cork are usually considered too informal for social areas.
Stairs Stairway flooring should be durable, feel warm underfoot and minimize sound. If the stairs lie between differently decorated areas, you may prefer a neutral color for the flooring.	For its sound absorption, warmth and wide price range, carpet is a common choice for stairways. Durable natural-fiber floorings offer an attractive alternative, and wood is also very popular (but can be noisy).	Linoleum is durable, but colder underfoot than other options. The manufactured feel of vinyl doesn't blend with many styles beyond kitchens and bathrooms.	Some natural-fiber coverings are dangerously coarse or slippery on stairs. Hard tiles may also be too slippery, and the stairway construction would likely need to be redesigned to accommodate them.
Bedrooms Comfort underfoot and good sound insulation tend to be the most important criteria for bedroom flooring. Durability and ease of maintenance are not as important as in other sites, and since your bedroom will be smaller than other living areas you may decide to choose luxury over cost-effectiveness.	Carpet and wood are both chosen for their versatility and good price range. Many people refinish existing wood floors in bedrooms, and use rugs for comfort. Leather offers a marvelous mix of comfort and luxury, but it is expensive.	Natural-fiber floors are welcoming, but prickly. Linoleum and cork are more natural than vinyl and can work well in bedrooms. Laminate is practical, but may feel too artificial.	Hard floors are only suitable for bedrooms in year-round hot climates. Vinyl is considered too artificial, and rubber too clinical for use in bedrooms.
Bathrooms The floor should be nonslip and able to cope with water. Warmth and comfort are also considerations. As bathrooms are often small, price is less important—this is one place you can be particularly extravagant.	Ceramic tiles with a slip-resistant surface are frequently laid to match wall tiles, and many people strip old softwood floorboards and paint them. (If the boards are laid only on joists, air will be able to circulate and prevent deterioration caused by moisture.) Vinyl and linoleum are comfortable and practical. Mosaic, marble and slate are chosen for water resistance and effect, but feel cold. Sealed cork is widely used for its warmth, softness and ease of maintenance.	Carpet is frequently installed, but moisture may cause deterioration. Hardwood boards laid over floorboards may warp.	Natural-fiber floors usually react badly to water. Laminate will deteriorate if water penetrates the joints. The rougher hard floors, terra-cotta for example, are not smooth enough underfoot, and will retain water on the surface. Hard floors in general, apart from ceramic and mosaic, may be too heavy for suspended wood subfloors on upper stories.
Children's rooms Cleanliness and safety are critical in children's rooms. The floor should be easy to maintain and forgiving on toys and knees.	Carpet is widely used in children's bedrooms, but will stain. Carpet also harbors dust that may give rise to allergies or asthma. Easy-to-clean resilient floorings such as rubber, linoleum, vinyl and cork are particularly suitable. Laminate is clean and fairly soft.	Wood is harder than laminate and may produce splinters.	Hard floors are uncomfortable and even dangerous for a child to fall on. Natural flooring is prickly, difficult to clean and, like carpet, may harbor dust and provoke allergies.

Can the subfloor take the weight?

One vital factor to consider when choosing your floor is whether the subfloor can support it. A concrete ground-level subfloor will be able to take any hard-tile floor, and the suspended concrete subfloors found in condos and apartment buildings should also be able to support a heavy flooring material. Be careful if you plan to install brick pavers or heavy floors such as limestone, sandstone or slate over a wood subfloor (especially if you plan to lay them in a mortar bed). These days, hard flooring materials are supplied in the form of tiles, rather than slabs, but they may still be too heavy to lay upstairs. Some floors may be available in thinner sections that put less of a burden on the subfloor: brick pavers, for example, are sold in a range of thicknesses, and are thinner than standard construction bricks. Ask a builder whether the subfloor complies with your local codes, and consider lighter alternatives such as ceramic.

Going green

Choosing "green" flooring not only creates a healthy home for you and your family, but also makes a big difference to the environment. Many people are concerned that chemicals used in the manufacture of products such as vinyl may trigger allergies, and prefer to source nontoxic flooring. Others are worried about the exhaustion of natural resources, and look for floors made from easily replenished or recycled materials. Increasingly, manufacturers are expanding their environmentally friendly ranges, offering ever more colors and designs to satisfy growing consumer demand. These are some of the greenest alternatives:

WOOD The most environmentally friendly wood products are recycled hardwood or softwood boards, composed of remilled wood salvaged from old properties. If you are buying new wood, check with your supplier that it is from a certified renewable source, and avoid tropical hardwoods, which are less likely to be managed in a sustainable way.

BAMBOO Actually a grass, not a tree, bamboo is harvested from managed plantations and will grow back in around four years. Harvesting bamboo does not destroy the habitats of endangered wildlife.

CORK Manufactured from the bark of a living tree, cork is the ideal sustainable material. The harvesting of cork bark stimulates rather than impedes the growth of the tree, and choosing cork will aid the survival of endangered Mediterranean cork forests.

LINOLEUM Made from linseed oil, wood flour, pine resin and ground limestone spread over a jute backing, linoleum is biodegradable and does not release toxic fumes.

RUBBER Bonded crumb rubber products are made from shredded tires. You can buy recycled rubber carpet padding, and also rubber flooring in the form of tiles or interlocking mats, which dispose of 7.5 tires for every 100 sq. ft. (9.3 sq. m) of flooring. Recycled rubber is usually found in a recreational or commercial context, but an increasing range of colors is making this a viable option for the home, too.

VINYL Chlorine-free vinyl tiles are available for those concerned about the toxic fumes that may be emitted by standard vinyl. It is also possible to buy vinyl tiles that include a percentage (up to 100 percent) of recycled PVC. These are usually seen in recreational or commercial settings, but manufacturers are working on creating products for the home.

CARPET The fibers of recycled carpet are made from polyethylene terephthalate (PET), recycled from soft-drink bottles. PET fiber processing does not require the consumption of fossil fuels and does not generate nitrous oxide. It does, however, dispose of around 36 used soft-drink bottles per square yard (0.8m) of carpet. These products are stain-resistant and very durable. Often coarse in appearance, they are usually seen in public areas, but they are now being refined for domestic use.

NATURAL-FIBER FLOORING The sale of sisal, seagrass, jute and coir enables Third World countries to benefit from their local sustainable resources. These products are biodegradable.

GLASS Old wine and beer bottles are now being transformed into glass floor tiles. The bubbling and cracking produced by the recycling process is considered to add interest to the floor.

Cost and difficulty

One of the main reasons why amateurs choose to lay floors is to save money, but the cost of materials must be balanced carefully with the difficulty of installation, otherwise the price of saving on professional labor might be a ruined floor. Carpet and vinyl are among the least expensive flooring materials, but when supplied in rolls (broadloom) or as sheets they are hard to maneuver and for that reason are also among the most difficult to fit. Linoleum and vinyl tiles, rather than sheet, are much more suitable for amateurs. Carpet can also be supplied as tiles, which may not be very good quality; however, broadloom is often sold with the cost of installation included. At the other end of the scale, terra-cotta tiles can be expensive to buy, but are relatively straightforward to install. Metal, marble, granite, glass and terrazzo floors are both expensive and very difficult to lay, and should be installed only by a professional.

When budgeting for your new floor, don't forget the hidden costs of installation. You will need to rent or buy tools, as well as obtain the required underlayments. Floors such as stone, terra-cotta, brick and cork will need to be sealed, and all hard floors require grouting, as well as caulking in wet areas. Check the list of tools and materials at the beginning of each section to establish exactly what you will need to complete the project.

You should also consider the cost of ongoing maintenance. Wood floors are often supplied prefinished, and these are simple to maintain, but untreated boards will need finishing with varnish, oil or wax, and you will have to apply further coats when the surface begins to wear off (usually at half-yearly intervals). Terra-cotta in particular requires repeated coats of wax polish to preserve its appearance and keep it waterproof, and any hard-tile floor that you have sealed yourself will benefit from additional coats of sealant. Suppliers of hard and resilient tiles will offer a selection of cleaning, enhancing and stripping products, which may be expensive and are not always necessary: water and household cleaning products, for example, will wash most tiled floors (with the particular exception of leather) as efficiently as a specialized cleaner. Before making any decisions, read the information regarding maintenance that is given for each type of floor.

RELATIVE LEVELS OF COST, EXPERTISE AND MAINTENANCE

These floors have been graded 1–5 for their relative cost and difficulty of installation (with 5 the most expensive and difficult). Cost may be expressed by a range of numbers, as most flooring materials are available in varying qualities. The maintenance column shows the level of ongoing upkeep required. Check also that your subfloor meets the requirements of the material (and consult a builder or contractor if you are unsure).

TYPE OF FLOORING	COST	DIFFICULTY	INSTALLATION	MAINTENANCE	RECOMMENDED SUBFLOOR
HARD FLOORS					
Brick	2–3	2–3	DIY	Medium	Concrete
Ceramic	2–4	3	DIY	Low	Concrete/Wood
Clay	3–4	3	DIY	Low	Concrete
Concrete (repairing)	1	1	DIY	Low	Concrete/Dirt
Glass	5	5	Expert	High	Suspended in a metal framework
Limestone/Sandstone	4–5	4	DIY	Low	Concrete
Marble/Granite	5	5	Expert	Low	Concrete
Metal	5	5	Expert	Medium	Concrete
Mosaic	2–4	2	DIY	Low	Concrete/Wood
Slate	3–4	3	DIY	Low	Concrete
Terra-cotta	3–4	3	DIY	Medium	Concrete
Terrazzo	5	5	Expert	Low	Concrete
RESILIENT FLOORS					
Cork	1–3	1	DIY	Low	Concrete/Wood
Leather	5	2	DIY	High	Concrete/Wood
Linoleum (sheet)	2–4	4	DIY/Expert	Low	Concrete/Wood
Linoleum (tiles)	2–4	1	DIY	Low	Concrete/Wood
Rubber	3–4	2	DIY	Medium	Concrete/Wood
Vinyl (sheet)	1–4	3	DIY/Expert	Low	Concrete/Wood
Vinyl (tiles)	1–4	1	DIY	Low	Concrete/Wood
SOFT FLOORS					
Carpet (broadloom)	1–5	5	DIY/Expert	Medium	Concrete/Wood
Carpet (tiles)	1–2	1	DIY	Medium	Concrete/Wood
Natural-fiber	2–4	4	DIY/Expert	Medium	Concrete/Wood
WOOD FLOORS					
Laminate	2–3	2	DIY	Low	Concrete/Wood
Wood (floating)	4–5	3	DIY	Low	Concrete/Wood
Wood (glued)	4–5	4	DIY/Expert	Low/Medium (depending on finish)	Concrete/Wood
Wood (nailed)	4–5	4	DIY/Expert	Low/Medium (depending on finish)	Concrete/Wood
Wood (renovation)	1–2	1	DIY	Low/Medium (depending on finish)	Concrete/Wood

Planning, design and layout

Once you've chosen your flooring material, you are ready to make decisions about color and design, and to consider the practicalities of how the floor will be laid out. Each floor will be available in a range of styles and colors, and widely varying looks can be achieved with the same type of flooring: a regularly jointed, smooth beech floor creates a contemporary effect, for example, while pickled oak boards, with randomly staggered joints, produce an old-world feel. Browse through interior decorating magazines and books, and visit your local suppliers to look at samples and ask for advice. In this book, the step-by-step instructions to laying each floor are preceded by photographs showing the floor in different room settings, as well as by information about available colors and designs, and ideas about how the flooring might work in your own home.

USEFUL TIPS
- Keep in scale: large tiles are generally best used in large rooms; small tiles in small rooms (although breaking this rule can achieve interesting results).
- Consider your other furnishings: a patterned carpet underneath a complex wallpaper may be too busy.
- Patterns and wood boards laid lengthwise will make a space seem longer; laid widthwise they will make the room seem wider but shorter.
- A bold geometric design will make a room appear more formal, and may make small rooms seem even smaller.
- Lighter shades help small rooms appear larger, while rich, dark tones create a more intimate environment.
- Remember texture: rough surfaces will create a rustic or casual feel; very glossy surfaces produce a more airy and sophisticated look.

Flooring transitions

Doorways often act as transitions between two types of flooring, and you may need to consider the color contrast at that point. Some people prefer their floors to simply butt up one against the other, but there are many designs of threshold moldings available that will marry floorings of different levels, colors or types. A simple wood, metal or plastic threshold can be nailed or screwed to the floor to provide a separation line between contrasting flooring materials; choose an appropriate thickness to match the flooring heights. Some thresholds, called reducers, have a sloping edge to ease the transition to a lower level of flooring. Threshold moldings are used particularly in the case of soft floorings, when a carpet bar, threshold or Z-bar binding strip is often attached to the floor before installation and then closed to grip the covering after it has been fitted (☞ page 125). You can also buy threshold moldings to fit at the top and bottom of stairs.

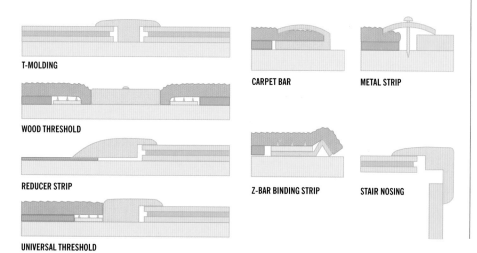

T-MOLDING

WOOD THRESHOLD

REDUCER STRIP

UNIVERSAL THRESHOLD

CARPET BAR

Z-BAR BINDING STRIP

METAL STRIP

STAIR NOSING

Mapping the site

The packaging will state the area covered by the flooring product you are buying, but you should also ask your supplier for advice about how much you require. You will need to make a detailed plan of the area you intend to finish. Measure the entire perimeter of the room, recording any recesses, steps or areas under built-in furnishings that you will be covering (inside closets or behind bathroom fixtures, for example). The plan should be drawn to scale on graph paper. Then calculate the total area of the site. The area of a simple room with no recesses can be determined by multiplying its length by its width. The area of a more complicated room, an L-shaped site, for example, or a bedroom with closets, must be calculated in segments.

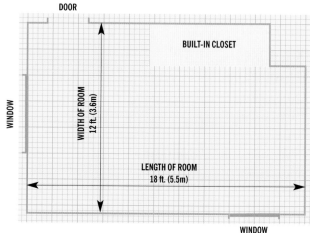

DOOR

BUILT-IN CLOSET

WINDOW

WIDTH OF ROOM
12 ft. (3.6m)

LENGTH OF ROOM
18 ft. (5.5m)

WINDOW

COMPARE THE LOOK

HARD FLOORS

Concrete
Increasingly popular, when finished by painting or waxing, for an industrial aesthetic.

Ceramic
A huge range of colors in gloss or matte, and usually glazed. Can be plain or patterned (many beautiful hand-painted designs are available).

Clay
Available in traditional earthy shades and bright modern colors. Can be glazed or unglazed.

Terra-cotta
Usually brick-red, orange or pink, in a variety of different shapes. Creates a warm and rustic effect.

Mosaic
Many brilliant or muted colors. The look can be contemporary or classical, and is limited only by your imagination.

Slate
A range of dramatically moody colors: dark greens, grays and purples. Often laid very closely spaced for a sophisticated effect.

Limestone/Sandstone
Many colors from white to near black, but often warm shades like honey. Tiles are closely laid, for an elegant contemporary feel, or more widely spaced for a rustic effect.

Brick
Fashionable and unusual, with a rustic or industrial feel.

Marble/Granite
Smooth, luxurious and classical, with great variety of patterning.

Terrazzo
Marble or granite chips set in concrete or resin produce an elegant, contemporary look.

Metal
Industrial, sleek and very contemporary.

Glass
Very stylish, adding translucency to a contemporary setting.

RESILIENT FLOORS

Vinyl
The greatest range of colors, patterns, motifs and feature strips of any floor. Many simulated wood and hard-floor effects, too, though these can be less successful than laminate.

Cork
Increasing choice of colors, but usually supplied in warm shades of brown ranging from honey to mahogany.

Linoleum
Many colors, patterns and motifs available, often with a marbled effect. Can look less artificial than vinyl. Fabulous designs may be custom-made.

Rubber
Many bright colors available, as well as various studded textures, for those who require a contemporary, industrial look.

Leather
The rich, dark colors of leather are at their best when lovingly waxed. Design choices center around different shapes of tile rather than colors.

SOFT FLOORS

Carpet
Can be smooth and sophisticated, luxuriously long-piled, or rough and casual to suit your tastes. Wide range of colors and patterns available. Carpet tiles offer scope for your creativity.

Natural-fiber
Interesting rough textures and pleasingly natural browns, greens and blues.

WOOD FLOORS

Wood
A great variety of different woods available, with colors ranging from near-white to the deepest brown-black. Can be rustic or sophisticated, traditional or contemporary, depending on the product selected. Wood finishes, such as stain or varnish, can completely change the look of a cheap softwood floor.

Laminate
Provides a more convincing imitation of wood than vinyl and greater choice of different wood effects. Also available in an increasing range of hard-floor simulations. The clean look of laminate adds brightness to an interior.

Calculating widths of roll and sheet flooring

Carpet, natural-fiber coverings and vinyl and linoleum sheet will be cut to the length required but are only available in certain widths. Buy a wider piece than you actually need in order to avoid seaming. If your room is even wider than the biggest width available, buy extra length and split and seam it to cover the missing width. Use your plan to establish where the seams will fall: you may wish to move them from a high-traffic or very visible area. When buying the product, you will need to add an extra 1 in. (2.5cm) for each seam on a vinyl or linoleum sheet, and an extra 3 in. (7.5cm) for each carpet or natural-fiber seam. Allow for around 2 in. (5cm) at each edge for trimming.

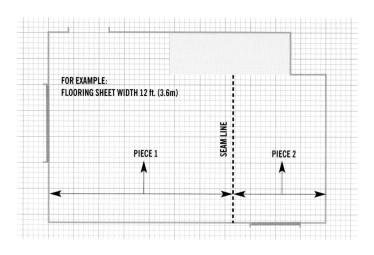

FOR EXAMPLE:
FLOORING SHEET WIDTH 12 ft. (3.6m)

SEAM LINE

PIECE 1   PIECE 2

LAYING OUT THE FLOOR

The temptation is to start laying out the floor along the straightest wall, and with sheet materials like carpet, vinyl and natural-fiber flooring, that's exactly how to begin. If you are laying wood or brick, however, you will first have to create a perfectly straight starting edge with a chalk line or mason's line. Tiles, on the other hand, must be laid from the center of the room.

The quarter method

This method can be used to lay out all tiles. If you wish to lay tiles in a staggered pattern, such as running bond, lay them out along one axis of the chalk cross only.

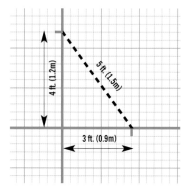

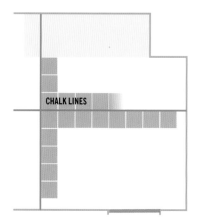

CHALK LINES

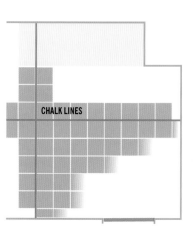

CHALK LINES

First measure and mark the midpoint of all four walls. Snap chalk lines joining opposite midpoints to create a cross running through the center of the site.

Check that the crossed lines form true right angles at the center by measuring 4 ft. (1.2m) along one line and 3 ft. (0.9m) along the other. If the lines are at a right angle, a diagonal line drawn between the two points will measure 5 ft. (1.5m). If it does not, adjust the lines.

Before setting any tiles in place, you will need to lay out the entire floor in a dry run. Start by laying rows of tiles dry along each of the four lines, working from the center to the walls, so that you have a cross of tiles the full length and width of the room. Don't forget to include spacers to mark grout lines, if required.

When you reach the walls, you will probably be left with spaces of less than a tile's width. If these are of differing sizes, or if any are less than the width of a half-tile, adjust the chalk lines until the layout is symmetrical with no spaces of less than a half-tile. Then finish laying out the floor. Begin with the cross, then fill in each quarter, working from the intersection to the walls.

Quantities of tiles

You can divide the total area of your site by the area of each tile to establish how many are required. This method does not, however, take into account the width of grout lines, which may be as much as ¾ in. (2cm). It also does not account for wastage at the edges, where you may have to discard cut pieces, as set tiles should not be less than half a tile wide. Plot all the tiles on your plan and adjust until the cut tiles around the edges are an equal measurement and not narrower than a half-tile width. Tiles can vary from batch to batch so buy them all at the same time (check that the packaging is marked with the same batch number), with at least 5 percent extra for spares.

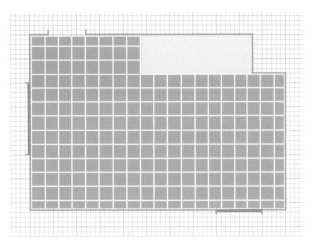

The border method

If you are installing a border of contrasting tiles, or a border feature strip, you will need to lay out the tiles so that the border dictates where the cut tiles will be. Before you find the center of the room, snap chalk lines around the room at the required distance from the walls. Then follow the quarter method described opposite, establishing the center from the border lines, rather than from the walls.

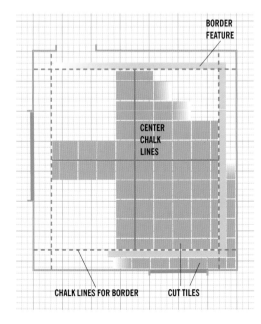

BORDER FEATURE

CENTER CHALK LINES

CHALK LINES FOR BORDER   CUT TILES

USEFUL TIP
Laying out the entire floor in a dry run gives you a chance to check its overall look, and make any adjustments (harmonizing any tonal variations, for example) before installation.

The diagonal method

If you want to lay tiles diagonally across the space, snap chalk lines along the two diagonals of the room to create a cross. Then proceed as for the quarter method, adjusting the lines until the right angles are square and the cut edge tiles are equal in width.

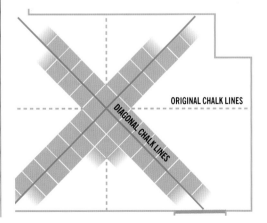

DIAGONAL CHALK LINES

ORIGINAL CHALK LINES

Planning a complex layout

If you are laying tiles or bricks, you may want to design a more complex layout, perhaps with a border, feature strips or a geometric design of contrasting colors such as checkerboard. A brick floor usually has a staggered layout, such as running bond, herringbone or basketweave, and mosaic is also often laid in patterns of varying complexity (if you are inexperienced, start with a simple design). Use graph paper to make a scale plan of the room, mapping out the design precisely in color, and follow this when buying different materials and laying out the floor.

The straight-line method

It is not necessary to find the center of the room when laying wood or laminate boards. Simply establish a straight starting line by snapping a chalk line parallel to the longest, straightest wall, at a distance of the width of a board plus the expansion gap (½ in. /1.25cm) plus the width of the tongue (unless this has been removed). Nailed boards are laid with tongues facing into the room, so in this case simply snap a chalk line ½ in. (1.25cm) away from the wall. If the wall is not straight, use a try square to establish a straight line at the correct distance from a corner. Extend this line along the floor with a straightedge, and use it as a guide when snapping the chalk line. Laid from a straight starting line, the long boards will naturally cover the room in an aligned way, and any unevenness around the edges caused by uneven walls can be filled later with wood filler or boards cut lengthwise, or covered by moldings.

Use your plan to establish whether the last row of boards will be very thin; if so, you can adjust the layout so there is an equal width of cut boards at either end of the room. If you are laying bricks, you will need to use a mason's line along the longest, straightest wall to provide both a straight starting edge and a height level. Again, map out the layout before starting to ensure you are not left with a thin strip of bricks at one edge.

Tools and materials

A basic toolkit will take you a long way, but you may also have to buy some specialized flooring tools. Expensive items, such as power cutting tools and electric sanders, or the hygrometer, linoleum roller, heat welder or seaming iron, can be rented from your supplier or local hardware store.

BASIC TOOLKIT

You will probably already have equipment such as a utility knife, a retractable tape measure, screwdrivers, standard and claw hammers, pliers, painter's tape, duct tape, and pencils and nonpermanent markers. To complete your basic flooring kit, you will also need some of the following items:

Chalk line Secure the hook at the end of the chalked string and extend the line over the floor to snap a straight line.

Carpenter's level A wood or metal bar with spirit level incorporated, used for establishing levelness. The longer the length the more accurate the measurement, so invest in a 4 ft. (1.2m) level, or rest a shorter level on a straightedge.

Straightedge A 5 ft. or 6 ft. (1.3m or 1.8m) length used to check that lines are straight, join up points and, in conjunction with a carpenter's level, establish levelness. A purchased straightedge, featuring measurements, is useful; alternatively, use a piece of planed wood, such as a baseboard.

Try square Two straightedges fixed at right angles, used for establishing perpendicular and for measuring.

Trowels A ⅛ in. (3mm) notched trowel can be used for spreading adhesive. Different sizes of trowels are available, but the ⅛ in. (3mm) size will do in all cases apart from where a very thin layer is needed.

Paint rollers and paintbrushes Use a standard paint roller for applying sealant and where a thin layer of adhesive is required. Both ¼ in. (6mm) and ½ in. (1.25cm) paintbrushes are suitable for working sealant into grout lines and applying wood finishes to edges.

Rubber mallet You can use a rubber mallet to tap hard tiles firmly into spread adhesive.

Cold chisel Used in conjunction with a hammer to split bricks, pull up old flooring, and so on.

Spacers Plastic or rubber tile spacers (often X-shaped) are available in a range of sizes, from around ¹⁄₁₆ in. (1.5mm) to ½ in. (1.25cm). They are placed at the corners of tiles to ensure consistent grout lines. You can make your own out of plywood or strips of packaging. Wood spacers are ½ in. (1.25cm) wedges that mark the expansion gap at the edges of the room.

ADDITIONAL TOOLS

Some flooring tasks require the use of more specialized tools.

Preparing the site

Pry bar Can be used for pulling up old flooring and removing moldings and baseboards.

Floor scraper Used to pull up old floor coverings.

Hygrometer A hygrometer records moisture levels to check for dampness.

Plasterer's trowel Used for smoothing down leveling compound or cement screed.

Jamb saw Trim door casings with a jamb saw if you have to adjust the height of doors.

Laying hard floors

There are many specialized hard-floor cutting tools. These are described in *Cutting hard tiles* (☛ pages 26–27). You may also need:

Brick trowel, mason's trowel and pointing trowel Brick and mason's trowels are used to mix and spread mortar. A pointing trowel is used to pack mortar into joints.

Grouting float This tool is used to transfer grout to the tiles and push it into the grout gaps.

Caulking gun Fitted with a cartridge of caulking to be applied around the base of walls and fixtures in order to waterproof edges.

Laying resilient floors

Linoleum knife Used for cutting linoleum and other thick resilient floorings, this knife has a curved blade that is stronger than a utility-knife blade. You can also fit linoleum-knife blades in your utility knife.

Heat welder Melts thin strips of linoleum called welding rod into the seams between sheets. Not recommended for use by the inexperienced.

Linoleum roller Roll resilient floors to remove air bubbles and press the covering firmly into the adhesive. Also used for rolling soft floorings. Check that the roller is perfectly clean before use.

SAFETY EQUIPMENT

Don't skimp on safety equipment, as handling some of the tools and materials can be dangerous. Always follow the safety instructions.

Strong rubber gloves Protect your hands from materials such as leveling compound, adhesive, sealant and varnish.

Safety glasses Protect the eyes from flying shards and splinters when using electric tools or scraping up old tiles.

Ear protectors Worn when using electric tools.

Face mask Prevents the inhalation of dust or fumes when sawing or working with materials such as leveling compound.

Laying wood floors

Fine-tooth handsaw, circular saw and wood bit A handsaw with fine, hard teeth cuts wood and laminate. A portable circular saw is faster. Attach a wood bit to your electric drill to drill pipe holes.

Tapping block This is struck gently with a hammer to knock boards into place.

Tapping bar Used to tightly pull in rows of boards that are difficult to reach.

Air nailer Used to drive nails into wood boards. A dangerous tool that should be handled with care.

Nail set Drive nails below the surface of the wood with a nail set and hammer.

Drum and edge sanders Use a drum sander for the room's center; an edge sander for the perimeter. Attach fine-, medium- or coarse-grade sandpaper, depending on the state of the boards. For light hand-sanding, wrap sandpaper around a block of wood.

Laying soft floors

Metal snips For cutting tackless strips to size.

Staple gun Attach padding to a wood subfloor with a staple gun.

Carpet shears Cut loop-pile carpet with carpet shears rather than a utility knife.

Seaming iron Used when seaming carpets to melt the adhesive on the hot-glue seaming tape.

Knee kicker Knock this device with your knee to stretch a soft covering.

Stair tool Used to tuck in carpet or natural-fiber flooring behind tackless strips.

FACE MASK

EAR PROTECTORS

SAFETY GLASSES

ADHESIVE TROWELS

CHALK LINE

COLD CHISEL

PLASTIC SPACERS

PRY BAR

ELECTRIC JAMB SAW

RUBBER MALLET

LINOLEUM BLADE FOR UTILITY KNIFE

HEAT WELDER

AIR NAILER

LINOLEUM KNIFE

METAL SNIPS

SEAMING IRON

NAIL SET

LINOLEUM ROLLER

SEAMING TAPE

STAPLE GUN

SOFT-FLOOR PADDING

WOOD FOAM UNDERLAYMENT

MATERIALS

New flooring is usually sold with a warranty, but this will be invalidated if you ignore the manufacturer's stipulations about the use of materials such as adhesive. Buy the recommended product and follow the instructions printed on the container. This book gives guidelines for using materials—recommending the depth of spread adhesive for example—but you should check that any advice matches the manufacturer's instructions. Your supplier will be able to guide you to suitable products. You do not have to buy every item offered by the manufacturer—not all special cleaning or enhancing products are necessary—but check the warranty before using alternatives.

Underlayment

Leveling compound Used to level a concrete subfloor. Supplied as liquid latex and latex powder, which are mixed together according to manufacturer's instructions. Not needed if the subfloor is to be covered by a wood floor or by a soft floor with padding, unless the concrete is in very bad condition.

Marine plywood To make a wood subfloor level and rigid, ¼ in. (6mm) marine plywood is recommended (sometimes ¾ in./2cm is required). This is not usually needed under wood floors or soft floors with padding. Marine plywood should be waterproof already, but paint it with diluted PVA adhesive before installation as a precaution. Exterior-grade plywood can be used if marine plywood is not available.

Cement backerboard A thin sheet of concrete and fiberglass used to provide a rigid surface for hard tiles laid on a wood subfloor. Marine plywood treated with diluted PVA adhesive will provide a similarly stable base (and is easier to install).

Foam underlayment Installed below a floating wood or laminate floor to take up unevenness, add bounce and extend the life of the floor. Sometimes supplied with a water-resistant coating to remove the need for a separate layer of waterproofing.

Polyethylene sheet and liquid damp-proof membrane (DPM) Two means of waterproofing the subfloor to protect the floor covering from moisture.

Acoustic panels These products combine a hard fiberboard backing with a layer of high-density compressed foam. Laid straight onto the subfloor, in place of plywood, they provide a hard, smooth surface as well as thermal and sound insulation, and increased fire protection.

Soft-floor padding Usually made from polyurethane foam, bonded polyurethane, rubber or fiber; manufacturers are also currently developing lightweight alternatives. Ask your supplier about the recommended padding for your type of soft floor.

Adhesive

Always follow the manufacturer's recommendations. Hard-tile adhesive can sometimes be used on a range of tiles, but adhesives for resilient coverings tend to be specific to each floor. Special adhesives are also produced for different types of wood board and for various soft floors. Discuss your needs with your supplier, as there are also different kinds of adhesive for different sites. Adhesive is supplied in various forms: ready-mix is the most convenient.

Mortar

Used to set some brick floors and as an alternative to adhesive for some hard tiles. Add water to ready-mix mortar until a creamy consistency is achieved. Liquid latex additive makes mortar more flexible (add about a half-cup to a half-bucketful of mortar).

Sealant

Unglazed tiles, and grouting on all floors, should be sealed to protect tiles from staining and waterproof the floor. Ask your supplier to recommend the appropriate product. Diluted PVA adhesive (which is simply white glue watered down to 1 part glue to 2 parts water) gives an extra coat of waterproofing to marine plywood before it is installed over the subfloor.

Grout

This is placed between tiles to hold them in place and waterproof the floor. There are different types of grout: your supplier will recommend a product suitable for your site. The best grouts are flexible and water-resistant. Grout is sold in a range of colors to match or contrast with your tiles.

Caulking

This is inserted between the flooring and the walls and base of fixtures where extra waterproofing is needed. Caulking is supplied as cartridges that are fitted into a caulking gun, and is available in a range of colors.

Seaming materials

Hot-glue seaming tape is used to join pieces of carpet. Welding rod is melted into linoleum seams.

Preparing the site

Before laying your new floor it is essential that you prepare the site properly. This includes removing the existing floor covering and, if necessary, repairing, strengthening and leveling the underlying subfloor. You may need to install waterproofing, and some floors require a layer of padding or foam underlayment. You may also want to lay special underlayment, such as acoustic panels, for sound insulation and as a fire-retardant. If you are laying wood or laminate, you will have to remove moldings and baseboards so that they can be replaced later to cover expansion gaps. Moldings and baseboards are also often removed when laying vinyl or linoleum sheet and replaced later to produce a neater edge. If the level of your new floor is higher than the old covering, you may have to trim existing doors and casings.

LAYING ON A WOOD SUBFLOOR

Many houses are built with suspended wood subfloors, especially upstairs. Pull up the existing floor covering and check the condition of the boards. If they are loose, sagging or rotten, replace the affected boards with new ones (☞ pages 116–117).

Leveling with marine plywood

It is recommended to reinforce floorboards with ¼ or ¾ in. (6mm or 2cm) sheets of marine plywood to provide a firm and level base for the floor covering. If the floorboards have already been reinforced with plywood, make sure it is thick enough for the flooring you intend to install (check the chapter on your chosen floor for the recommended thickness). You may first need to lift the plywood to examine the floorboards below and sand them level if necessary. Remove any protruding nails or screws, as these could cause lumps in the new flooring. Smooth dents in the plywood with leveling compound (see opposite), and check that the floor is absolutely level using a carpenter's level.

If you are buying new plywood to install, get the lumber yard to cut it into sheets sized 4 x 2 ft. (1.2 x 0.6m). Use nails or screws that are no longer than the width of the subfloor plus plywood to avoid accidentally drilling into pipes or cables.

Step 2
Starting from the longest wall, nail or screw sheets onto the floorboards at 6 in. (15cm) centers around the edges and 10 in. (25cm) centers elsewhere. Butt sheets tightly together, and do not align the seams with floorboard joints. Cut sheets with a circular saw to fit at the edges, including notches for doorways and other obstructions.

Step 3
Check that the plywood is level using a carpenter's level and straightedge. Drive protruding nail or screw heads below the surface of the plywood with a nail set. Fill any gaps with leveling compound.

Step 1
In a bucket, mix water with PVA adhesive (1 part adhesive to 2 parts water). Paint a coat of diluted adhesive onto the side of the panels that will be laid onto the subfloor. Allow to dry for about 3 hours. This provides an extra coat of waterproofing.

Installing acoustic panels
If you want to install acoustic panels, which offer greater sound insulation than conventional underlayments, and also provide a particularly level, rigid base for the floor, fix them to the subfloor in place of plywood. Acoustic panels are thicker than plywood, so check whether you need to trim doors and make any adjustments before laying the floor. Installation systems vary, so ask your supplier for advice and follow the manufacturer's instructions.

Removing the existing floor

You can lay new flooring onto an existing hardwood or hard-tile floor (if it is stable and free of moisture), but this may raise the floor height unacceptably. If you leave old tiles in place, level them with leveling compound to a depth of ⅛ in. (3mm). Soft and resilient floors should not be left in place as they may deteriorate under the new floor (hire a professional to remove flooring that you suspect may contain asbestos). Cut resilient and soft flooring into strips with a utility knife, and pull it up, using a floor scraper if necessary. Remove tackless strips with a pry bar. Knock out hard tiles with a cold chisel and hammer or pull them up with a spade or floor scraper (wear safety goggles). You can remove plywood underlayment along with the covering. Set a circular saw to the depth of the underlayment plus flooring (do not cut into the subfloor). Open a cutting path on hard-tile floors with a cold chisel and hammer.

WARNING

VINYL FLOORING IN PRE-1980s HOMES MAY CONTAIN ASBESTOS. HIRE A PROFESSIONAL TO REMOVE OLD FLOORING IF YOU SUSPECT THAT IT MAY CONTAIN ASBESTOS.

LAYING ON A CONCRETE SUBFLOOR

If you live in an old property, you might pull up a ground-level floor to find there's no concrete subfloor below at all. In this case, you will need to build one yourself (☛ page 21). If the subfloor is badly damaged, you will have to repair it before applying leveling compound (☛ pages 20–21). If you are laying a leather or nailed wood floor, you will need to attach ¾ in. (2cm) marine plywood treated with diluted PVA adhesive (see opposite) to the concrete using the recommended adhesive, allowing it to dry as instructed. In all cases, remember to check for moisture.

Applying leveling compound

If you are laying a tiled floor with adhesive, a soft floor without padding or if the surface is very uneven, level a concrete subfloor with a mixture of liquid latex and latex powder called leveling compound. Always wear a mask, gloves and safety glasses while blending and applying the mixture, and keep the windows open, as the ingredients will give off fumes. Whisk the quantities advised by the manufacturer in a bucket, stirring until the powder is absorbed and you have a smooth paste without any lumps.

DEALING WITH MOISTURE

Waterproofing materials are available from building suppliers in the form of a polyethylene sheet or liquid damp-proof membrane, installed directly onto a concrete or wood subfloor. Upper floors are not affected by rising moisture, so you will not need to waterproof here, but it is always worth installing waterproofing under wood or laminate floors (even upstairs) to avoid invalidating the manufacturer's warranty.

Before installing a new floor, it is vital to test a ground-level concrete subfloor for moisture, especially if you have an older house (concrete used to be poured onto the ground without any form of waterproofing). A hygrometer rented from your building supplier will register the level of moisture in the floor. Alternatively, simply lay a heavy cooking pan on the floor overnight, and check underneath in the morning. If you find a dark patch on the concrete, then moisture is present. Another simple test is to tape down a 12 in. (30cm) square of clear plastic on the floor, and leave it overnight. If the floor is damp, there will be condensation on the plastic in the morning.

HYGROMETER

Step 1
Vacuum or sweep thoroughly. Scrub the floor clean and leave until dry. Then pour out the leveling compound to a depth of around ⅛ in. (3mm). Start in the farthest corner from the exit and work toward the door.

Step 2
Smooth out the leveling compound with a plasterer's trowel. The floor will take at least 24 hours to dry properly—do not attempt to lay the main flooring until the leveling compound is completely dry.

Step 1
If you find evidence of moisture, install a polyethylene sheet (suitable for waterproofing) or liquid damp-proof membrane before taking any further action. Cover the subfloor with the sheet, overlapping joints by 2 in. (5cm) and sealing with duct tape.

Step 2
Leave at least a 1 in. (2.5cm) overlap up the walls, to be trimmed back with a utility knife later. Liquid damp-proof membrane is simply applied with a paint roller and left to dry for 2 hours. Install other underlayments over the damp-proof membrane.

REMOVING BASEBOARDS AND MOLDINGS

Baseboards and moldings are removed for three reasons. First, they can be replaced later to create a neat edge to thin flooring, particularly sheet vinyl and linoleum. (Tiles are easier to cut to fit at room edges, so most people prefer to avoid the disruption caused by removing moldings and baseboards.) Second, they can be replaced to hide the ½ in. (1.25cm) expansion gap required around the edge of wood and laminate floors. Third, baseboards and moldings help to hold down floating wood and laminate floors. Baseboards are difficult to remove without damaging the wall, so you may want to leave them in place and hide the expansion gap simply by installing moldings.

Step 1

Lever moldings and baseboards off the wall with a pry bar and cold chisel. Take care not to damage them (unless you have bought replacements to match the floor).

Step 2

Replace baseboards and moldings in their original position with adhesive or finish nails (using the same holes as before). You may need to cut a strip off the bottom edge with a handsaw to accommodate the new floor height. If you are installing new baseboards or moldings, cut them to length with a handsaw, and use adhesive or finish nails to attach baseboards to the wall and moldings to the baseboards.

LEVEL OF DIFFICULTY

●○○○○

Small cracks and holes in a concrete subfloor are not hard to fill, but you must ensure the surface of the new concrete is level with the rest of the floor.

REPAIRING A CONCRETE SUBFLOOR

A concrete subfloor with lots of cracks and holes, rather than just a rough surface, should be repaired before leveling compound is applied. Mortar for repairs can be bought ready-mixed from your building suppliers.

Golden rules

• Most cracks will be superficial, but call in a professional for advice if you find a deep crack or a long crack running across the room.

• Wear safety glasses and gloves when opening up cracks with the cold chisel. Wear a mask, gloves and safety glasses when working with leveling compound.

Toolbox

1 COLD CHISEL
2 HAMMER
3 PAINTBRUSH (OF A SIZE APPROPRIATE FOR WIDTH OF CRACKS)
4 POINTING TROWEL
5 WOOD BATTEN

Materials

6 READY-MIX MORTAR
7 PVA ADHESIVE
8 LEVELING COMPOUND

Step 1

Insert a cold chisel into the crack, at an angle of around 60 degrees to the floor, and knock firmly with a hammer. This opens up the crack and provides increased gripping surface for the mortar.

Step 2

Prime the crack with a coat of PVA adhesive (white glue), diluted 1 part adhesive to 2 parts water (or according to the manufacturer's instructions). Apply the adhesive with a paintbrush. The adhesive will help the mortar grip the surface of the crack.

Step 3

Stir diluted PVA adhesive into the mortar mix until a buttery consistency is achieved. To avoid the mixture setting in the bucket, mix no more than you can use in an hour. Start with a half-bucketful.

TRIMMING DOORS

You may need to trim doors to fit over the new height of the floor. Do this before installation, when you have clear access. Lay out the flooring dry under the door and add an extra ⅛ in. (3mm) for clearance, marking the new level on the door and door casing. Then take the door off its hinges, score a cutting line with a utility knife, and cut with a circular saw or handsaw. You will also need to trim the door casing, using a handsaw or jamb saw. When rehanging the door, rest it on a wedge such as a large screwdriver laid on the floor while you reinsert the first couple of hinge pins.

Step 4
Press mortar into the crack with a pointing trowel. Use the edge of the trowel to level it off with the surface of the floor. Skim off any excess before the mortar dries. Leave to dry for at least 3 hours.

Step 5
To fill a wide crack, use a wood batten to level the repair (rather than a trowel as shown in Step 4). Move the batten from side to side as you pull it toward you. Sweep and vacuum the whole floor to remove dust and debris before applying leveling compound.

Heating your floor
Using your floor as a giant radiator can be a great idea, especially if you want to combine the spectacular effect of tiled stone flooring with the comfort of one of the warmer coverings. "Radiant" underfloor heating, which is supplied through a network of underfloor pipes or by wire-mesh matting, will add considerably to the cost of the installation, but this sort of energy-efficient heating can save more than 25 percent on your heating bill. All floors can accommodate modern underfloor heating, but ask the manufacturer for guidelines.

Finishing a concrete floor
If you would like a painted concrete floor for an industrial look, finish the floor with cement rather than leveling compound. Add water to cement mix until you achieve a creamy consistency, then smooth it over the concrete to a thickness of ⅛ in. (3mm), using a plasterer's trowel. Apply a generous coat of masonry sealer, and leave overnight to dry. You will then be able to paint the cement using floor paint (a wide range of colors is available). Allow each coat to dry overnight. The floor can also be waxed by applying liquid wax polish with a paint roller and then buffing with a cloth (or hire an electric floor polisher). Test a small area to check how slippery the floor will be before finishing the entire room.

Laying your own concrete subfloor
Occasionally it may be necessary to build an entirely new concrete subfloor, if you are renovating an old property, for example. Start by removing loose dirt and waterproofing the floor with polyethylene sheet (☛ page 19). Then stretch out a mason's line at the level of what will be the finished concrete floor. This will vary, but an average concrete floor is around 4 in. (10cm) thick. In a wheelbarrow, add water to ready-mix concrete and stir with a shovel until the mixture is flexible. Start in the far corner of the room by pouring out enough of the mix to cover approximately 2 sq. yd. (1.65 sq. m). Then work toward the exit, spreading the concrete with a pointing trowel to the correct depth. Wet a plasterer's trowel to gently smooth the surface. As you go, check the floor level using a carpenter's level. You must allow sufficient time for the floor to dry before installing any floor covering: at least 28 days (1 week per 1 in./2.5cm of depth) and up to 60 days if you are laying wood or laminate. After this time, check for moisture using a hygrometer or the saucepan method (☛ page 19). If no moisture is present, add a layer of leveling compound (☛ page 19).

HARD FLOORS

Tough and full of character, there's a hard floor to suit every setting, whether you want antique terra-cotta for a rustic kitchen or closely set, machine-cut slate to add glamor to an urban dwelling. These floors are always striking and are surprisingly straightforward to install (remember, however, that heavier tiles, such as sandstone and limestone, are very difficult for the amateur to cut and maneuver). Ceramic is probably the hard floor most often laid by nonprofessionals, and a correspondingly dazzling choice of colors and patterns is available. The truly sophisticated may wish to consider marble, granite, terrazzo, metal or glass; these floors are too difficult for amateurs to install, so make sure you call in the professionals to avoid costly mistakes.

Installing hard floors

The key feature of many hard floors, such as limestone, slate or brick, is that they tend to be very heavy—so it is important to check that the subfloor can take the weight. Laying hard flooring can be more complicated than installing other floors since it is often difficult to cut, and you will almost always have to grout and seal the floor (even if you are using glazed tiles it is still essential to seal grout lines).

How suitable is the subfloor?

Ground-level subfloors are usually concrete, or wood laid over concrete, and should be able to support the weight of any hard floor. An upper story may well have suspended wood subfloors, which may not be able to take the load of heavier materials.

Upper stories in condominium buildings, however, may have suspended concrete subfloors, which are much stronger. Always ask your supplier for advice.

Do not install hard tiles directly onto a wood subfloor since movement of the wood may result in cracking. A layer of ¼ in. (6mm) marine plywood treated with diluted PVA adhesive will provide a waterproof, stable base for tiles. Some installers, however, prefer to use cement backerboard. These concrete and fiberglass panels are attached to the floor with tile adhesive and screws. Ensure joints are staggered and not in line with subfloor joints. Leave ⅛ in. (3mm) gaps between panels and ¼ in. (6mm) gaps at the walls, and fill these with adhesive. Then seal joints between panels with fiberglass tape embedded in the adhesive.

TECHNIQUES FOR HARD FLOORS

Sort hard tiles before laying them out to harmonize variations in tone, size and thickness. Before installation, lay out the whole floor dry to check the overall effect—you might want to alter the position of some tiles if they stand out as being a slightly different color or shape. It's also essential to first lay out the floor dry when working with any geometric, linear or repeating pattern. Before you start, make a plan of your floor layout on graph paper, including any design (☞ pages 12–15). If you want to install a border of contrasting tiles, lay out the tiles following the border method (☞ page 15).

Adhesive or mortar?

Adhesive is simpler to use than mortar as it is supplied ready-mixed and the precise quantity for the area can be applied straight from the container. Mortar must be mixed with water in a bucket, sets faster than adhesive and is not recommended for use on a wood subfloor (mortar may rot wood). Mortar is cheaper than adhesive, however, and if you are confident in handling it, it can be quicker to use. It is best used for large, heavy stone tiles, and also for brick, when the mortar has to support a large number of bulky items. Adhesive is more convenient for other floors. Consult your supplier about the recommended bonding material for your particular floor and site.

HARD-TILE ADHESIVE

MORTAR MIX

Spreading the bond

Step 1
A plastic spreader is supplied with adhesive; alternatively, buy a ⅛ in. (3mm) notched trowel for spreading adhesive, and a mason's or brick trowel for mortar. Do not spread more adhesive or mortar than you can use in an hour, or it will set.

USEFUL TIP
It's easier to use extra adhesive or mortar to bring thin tiles up to the level of thick tiles than the other way around, so lay thicker tiles first, and adjust for the thinner tiles as you go.

Step 2
Push adhesive or mortar over the area with the smooth edge of the spreader or trowel.

Step 3
If you are spreading adhesive, "comb" it with the trowel's notched edge to create furrows. Mortar is not combed, but spread smoothly. Compensate for differences in thickness of tiles by increasing or decreasing the amount of adhesive or mortar used.

Spacing and grouting

Hard tiles are usually spaced and grouted. This is partly to hold them in place, partly to waterproof the floor and partly because natural stone tiles are rarely so regular that their edges would make a perfect fit without gaps. Grouting spaces vary according to the effect desired. The minimum joint is usually about ⅛ in. (3mm), which creates a precise, contemporary look for modern tiles such as ceramic. Some floors, such as terra-cotta, are less exacting in design, and the grouting gaps can be as wide as ¾ in. (2cm). Remember that very wide grouting may crack. Sandstone and limestone can be spaced either tightly or loosely, depending on taste and the shape of the tile. Most hard floors need joints of ¼–½ in. (6mm–1.25cm). Bricks, however, are often laid butted up without spaces. Always leave at least ⅛ in. (3mm) for grouting at the edges of the room.

If you have experience in laying floors, you may be able to space tiles by eye, especially when laying heavy tiles that will not move out of place. Otherwise, use spacers to regulate the gaps and keep the tiles from moving while you are laying them out dry. You can buy plastic spacers ranging in width from about 1⁄16–½ in. (1.5mm–1.25cm), or make your own out of bits of wood, or even use strips torn from the tile packaging.

PLASTIC TILE SPACERS

Step 1
Don't grout until you are sure that the adhesive or mortar has set properly (leave adhesive overnight and mortar for at least three hours). Use ready-mix waterproof, flexible grout. Mix it in a small container, adding water until you achieve a buttery consistency. Work with quantities of about 1 pint (0.5L) to prevent the grout from drying up in the container (you can increase the quantity as you gain confidence). Stone and brick floors are grouted with mortar mix.

Step 2
Press grout firmly into the joints using a rubber grouting float—the more compacted the grout is, the harder it will set. Do not allow excess grout to set on the surface of the tiles: wipe it off with a damp cloth or sponge. Wipe only once to avoid pulling grout out of the joints.

Step 3
Pressing down firmly on the grout lines with a small wooden dowel about ½ in. (1.25cm) in diameter will give an attractive finish and ensure channels for water to run in when the floor is washed. Then polish off any remaining smears of grout with a clean, damp cloth or sponge.

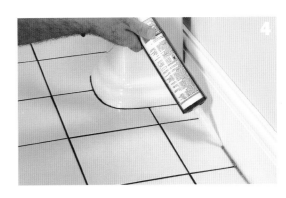

Step 4
If you are laying a floor in a kitchen, bathroom or other wet area, you will need to seal the gaps around the edges of the floor with caulking, applied with a caulking gun. Brick, however, looks better simply grouted at the edges with ready-mix mortar.

Sealing the tiles

Hard tiles are supplied glazed or unglazed. Clay tiles can be either, while ceramic and mosaic are normally glazed. Terra-cotta, stone and slate tiles are usually unglazed. Unglazed porous tiles must be sealed to prevent stains or spills penetrating the tile surface (slate is naturally waterproof, and does not usually need sealing). Sealing is not required for glazed tiles, as nothing can permeate the glaze, but the grout on any floor should be sealed to give it extra waterproofing. This is impractical in the case of mosaic, where there are hundreds of tiny grout lines, so be sure to use a good waterproof grout.

Step 1
Sweep or vacuum the floor before sealing. You can also wipe with a damp, clean cloth to remove dust.

Step 2
Use a paint roller to apply sealant in long strokes and consistent direction. Leave overnight to dry (drying times depend on ambient temperature and the porosity of the tiles and grout).

Step 3
If the tiles are glazed, seal only the grout lines, using a ½ in. (1.25cm) paintbrush. Try not to drop sealant onto the tiles, and wipe up any spills immediately with a clean cloth.

Cutting hard tiles

It is likely that the tiles you buy will not fit your room exactly and you will need to cut edge tiles to fit. When using large, expensive tiles it is worth calculating exactly how much cutting is needed, as offcuts can be used to prevent waste. Some hard tiles, such as ceramic or mosaic, can be cut easily using a tile cutter or tile nippers. Other tiles, such as slate, clay, limestone and sandstone, are harder to cut, and shaping them around corners, pipes and vents requires the use of more powerful tools. Items such as tile cutters, nippers and angle grinders are not expensive to buy, and you can also rent cutting tools from building suppliers, tool rental and tile shops. Use a straightedge or metal ruler to provide a straight line when scoring or marking tiles for cutting, and a try square to mark lines at 90 degrees to the edges. Rough edges can be smoothed with a tile file or sanding block (with coarse-grade sandpaper), or by rubbing the tile with the broken pieces of another tile.

Golden rules

- Wear a mask, safety glasses, gloves and ear protection when using power tools.
- Ensure that tiles to be cut are firmly secured in a vise or similar clamp.

USING THE CUTTING TOOLS

Tile cutter
Snap ceramic tiles in half with a tile cutter, which combines a scoring device and lever for snapping. Run the scorer up and down the tile, pressing gently on the lever. Then position the snap mechanism at the top of the scored tile, and press down firmly.

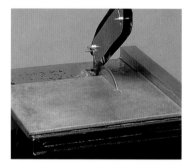

Diamond wheel cutter
If you are cutting many very hard tiles like slate, clay, limestone or sandstone, consider renting a diamond wheel cutter. This is a mechanized tile-cutting saw with a circular blade lubricated by water (change water frequently to prevent clogging). You will still need an angle grinder for curves and corners.

Angle grinder
An angle grinder fitted with a stone-cutting disk is the best tool to use for cutting corners and curves from clay, terra-cotta, slate, limestone and sandstone tiles, and also from bricks. Work slowly and carefully into your marked outline. Practice on scrap pieces first.

Diamond tile scorer, cold chisel and hammer
You can snap brick, as well as slate or terra-cotta tiles (if they are not too thick), with a diamond tile scorer and cold chisel. Score the surface of the tile or brick with a diamond tile scorer and then break it in two with a cold chisel and hammer. Practice on scrap tiles first.

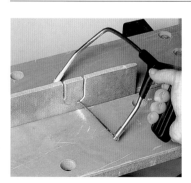

Hand tile saw
Ceramic tiles can also be cut using a hand tile saw, which is essentially a coping or fret saw. This is a useful tool if you have only a few cuts to make, but can be slow to use otherwise. The more expensive type of hand tile saw has a metal frame, and is less prone to flexing than saws with a plastic frame. You can also buy tile saw blades to fit your hacksaw.

HOLE-CUTTING
DRILL ATTACHMENTS

Drill with masonry bit
Use an electric drill with a masonry bit to create tight curves for pipes or curved walls. Drill the area to be removed, and then smooth with a half-round file. Also available are hole-cutting drill attachments designed for ceramic tiles, which produce a smooth hole that does not need filing. When fitting, you may have to split the tile in half across the center of the hole, and then lay the halves so that they meet around the pipe.

USEFUL TIP
Before cutting a hard tile, mark the area to be discarded by shading it with a pencil or felt-tip pen. This will help you avoid cutting too far into the area to be used.

Cutting edge tiles

A tiled floor should be laid out dry before fixing. Cut edge tiles at this stage. When you reach the edge of the room, place a tile on top of the last whole tile and push it over the empty space until it reaches the wall. Insert spacers between tile and wall to mark what will be the grouting gap. Now mark a cutting line onto the bottom tile, adding the extra width of a tile spacer as you draw (to allow for grouting on this side of the tile). Lift out the lower tile and cut along the line to make the edge tile. Alternatively, simply measure the width of the empty space, subtract the width of two grouting gaps, and mark a cutting line onto the tile. A try square will enable you to draw true lines.

Tile nippers
Tile nippers can be used to cut complicated shapes, such as holes for pipes, from ceramic tiles, and to split mosaic tesserae. If you are cutting an L-shape, score the edges of the shape with your tile cutter, but don't snap them. Then use the nippers to remove tile from between the score lines. If you are cutting a curve, mark the curve with a pen, then score a straight line from each end point of the curve, and snap this off as usual. Nibble out the remaining part of the curve with the nippers.

Cutting corner tiles

Step 1
Corner cuts are simply straight-edge cuts performed twice on one tile. Make the first cut as for an edge tile (see *Cutting edge tiles*, above).

Step 2
Then place the cut tile on the floor and position another tile on top to indicate the line for the second cut (see *Cutting edge tiles*, above). Remember to allow for grouting gaps.

Using a template

You can use a card or paper template to mark the shape of a pipe, complicated corner or curve onto a tile, and then cut out the shape using nippers, a tile saw or an angle grinder.

Step 1
Cut a piece of card to the size of the edge space. Lay the card in place, and mark the position of the center of the pipe.

Step 2
Fold the card on the pipe-center mark. Then position it with its edge flush to the wall and mark the depth of the pipe from the wall. You now have the outer dimensions of the pipe.

Step 3
Cut the card up the center mark to the pipe depth, then snip from the side marks to the center mark following the shape of the pipe.

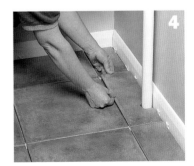

Step 4
Trace around the card template onto the tile, using a pencil (on unglazed tiles) or felt-tip pen (on glazed tiles). Cut out the shape and fit the tile into position.

Ceramic and clay

PROPERTIES AT A GLANCE
(*low, **medium, ***high)
• LOW MAINTENANCE ***
• WATER RESISTANCE ***
• HARD WEARING ***
• HEAT RETENTION *
• SOUND INSULATION *

A wide range of colors, patterns and shapes makes ceramic and clay tiles flexible in design, and suitable for both traditional and contemporary settings. Both are manufactured "stone," being made of, respectively, refined and unrefined clay, but ceramic tiles are lighter and smaller than clay, and tend to produce an effect that is more precise and polished than the rougher, more earthy appearance of clay tiles. They have similar qualities, however, being durable and cold to the touch (consider radiant underfloor heating if you live in a cool climate). Both sorts of tile are less porous than terra-cotta, the other manufactured stone, meaning that they require less maintenance.

Ceramic tiles are usually supplied glazed, and clay tiles are sometimes glazed. This can make them simpler to install than other stone tiles, as it is not necessary to seal the surface of an unglazed tile during installation—only the grout must be sealed. (Unglazed tiles, however, must be sealed during installation to make them properly waterproof.) Thanks to their water resistance, clay tiles are particularly popular in kitchens, while ceramic tiles are often found in bathrooms. Ceramic is valuable for use in upstairs bathrooms since, unlike other stone, it is always light enough to be laid on a suspended wood subfloor. You can buy matching ceramic wall tiles, as well as ceramic floor tiles with a nonslip surface. A standard ceramic tile is cheaper than clay, but the durability of the tiles means that both are an economical option.

Bear in mind that the closely spaced contemporary look of ceramic demands a precision of installation that is not easy to achieve. Use spacers to ensure consistent joints or buy "self-

Above: These modern ceramic floors reproduce the geometric patterning of nineteenth-century encaustic tiles. Original examples of these highly decorative floors can still be found in Victorian homes and American brownstones.

Designing the floor

Ceramic, of all the hard tiles, offers the most choice to the designer. Colors range from earth tones to the brightest primaries, in various matte or gloss finishes, and the shapes available include octagons, triangles and diamonds as well as squares and rectangles in many different sizes. There's great scope for combining sizes and shapes: perhaps by installing strips of smaller, patterned tiles as a border, or fitting diamond or square inset tiles at the corners of each tile to create a strong grid pattern over the floor. The aligned, glossy appearance of a ceramic floor usually suits a contemporary interior, but there are other looks too: antique-style patterned tiles in dusty colors will create a nineteenth-century feel. At the top end of the market, unique tiles can be handmade to suit your tastes.

Clay tends to be supplied in earth tones, and is usually rougher to the touch than ceramic, although glossy finishes and more vivid colors are also available. Traditional square clay tiles look wonderful in an old-fashioned kitchen, but you can also achieve a more sophisticated, modern effect by combining different sizes of tile in a formal pattern.

Right: Squares in two sizes and rectangles are used here to produce a grid design. The subtle coloring of the tiles prevents the arrangement from being overpowering.

Above: Bathrooms tend to be the smallest rooms in the house, so are great for trying out ideas. Why not go wild with the brightest ceramics you can find!

HARD FLOORS

spacing" ceramic tiles, with built-in lugs (protuberances that automatically space the tiles for grouting). You must also take special care when laying ceramic tiles (which are lighter than clay and so more prone to movement) that the subfloor is rigid and level. Clay is often laid closely spaced, too, but these tiles also suit a more rustic look, which is easier to achieve (but remember that clay is much harder to cut than ceramic).

Maintenance

Sweep regularly or vacuum. Clean off dirt with a wet mop, using diluted household detergent. Metal brushes can permanently mark the floor, so if you need to scrub, use a brush with nylon or natural bristles. If you have sealed the tiles yourself, treat them to a further coat of sealant every 6 to 12 months.

Advantages

- Very durable.
- Easy to maintain.
- Water-resistant (if correctly sealed).
- Wide range of colors and patterns available.
- Particularly suitable for kitchens, bathrooms and hallways.

Disadvantages

- Cold and hard underfoot.
- Tiles can smash easily during transit or installation.

Left: At the top end of the market, clay and ceramic tiles are hand-painted to order. Your floor can be as individual as your budget permits.

Above: Create a pattern within a pattern using inset tiles in a boldly contrasting color.

Left: These ceramic tiles have been produced with a slate-effect finish. Easier to handle than natural stone, ceramic that resembles limestone, sandstone or slate is a good choice if you are not comfortable working with the real thing.

Right: White tiles laid with black inset tiles at the corners create a classic look that seems never to go out of style.

Left: A random combination of colors, shapes and textures can give your floor the look of an abstract painting.

Right: White grout on red highlights the intricate layout of the tiles, giving a contemporary look to traditional red clay tiles. A brown or black grout would be less prominent, producing a more old-fashioned and warm appearance.

Laying a ceramic or clay floor

LEVEL OF DIFFICULTY

●●●○○

Ceramic tiles are lighter than other hard floor tiles and relatively easy to handle, but their installation demands precision. Clay tiles are heavier and harder to cut, but may be laid with looser joints, if desired.

Toolbox

1 CHALK LINE
2 TILE SPACERS
3 PAINTER'S TAPE
4 TILE CUTTER, TILE SAW AND TILE NIPPERS (FOR CERAMIC TILES)
5 ANGLE GRINDER/DIAMOND WHEEL CUTTER (FOR CLAY TILES)
6 MASONRY BIT AND HALF-ROUND FILE
7 ⅛ IN. (3MM) NOTCHED TROWEL
8 RUBBER MALLET
9 CARPENTER'S LEVEL
10 STRAIGHTEDGE
11 PLIERS
12 GROUTING FLOAT
13 DOWEL/GROUTING TOOL
14 CLEAN CLOTHS/SPONGES
15 ½ IN. (1.25CM) PAINTBRUSH/ PAINT ROLLER
16 CAULKING GUN (FOR WET AREAS)
17 VACUUM CLEANER/ SOFT BRUSH OR BROOM

Materials

18 CERAMIC/CLAY FLOOR TILES
19 CARD/KRAFT PAPER
20 CERAMIC/CLAY FLOOR TILE ADHESIVE
21 GROUT
22 TILE SEALANT
23 CAULKING (FOR WET AREAS)

Before you begin laying your ceramic or clay floor, remove existing floor coverings, and ensure that the subfloor is clean and smooth. Level concrete floors with leveling compound and cover wood floorboards with ¼ in. (6mm) marine plywood treated with diluted PVA adhesive (☛ pages 18–21 for detailed instructions). Make a floor plan to calculate how many tiles you need, and map out any pattern to ensure an even layout (☛ pages 12–15). Use tile spacers to achieve consistent joints between tiles, especially when installing ceramic, which should be laid with precisely spaced, narrow joints. "Self-spacing" ceramic tiles, with protruding lugs, are also available. If laying thick clay tiles, you might find it easier to make your own spacers from lengths of plywood or cardboard, rather than using the shorter plastic spacers.

Golden rules

• Prepare the site before starting (☛ pages 18–21). Take special care to ensure a rigid base for ceramic tiles.
• Buy all materials at the same time to guarantee consistency and availability.
• Ask your supplier for advice, and follow the manufacturer's instructions.
• Work safely. Ventilate the room well and wear strong rubber gloves when working with adhesive, sealant, grout or caulking. Wear a mask, safety glasses, gloves and ear protection when using power tools, and ensure that tiles to be cut are secured firmly.

INSTALLING CERAMIC OR CLAY TILES

Preparing the tiles

Sort the tiles for variations in color and pattern, and stack them in piles placed conveniently around the room. Take care when handling the tiles, especially ceramic, as they can smash easily. Before you start, mark two chalk lines at right angles across the center of the room, to act as guides in laying out the floor, and adjust according to the quarter method (☛ page 14). If you would like a border of contrasting tiles, start by laying this out first (☛ page 15).

Step 1
Lay the tiles dry along the adjusted chalk lines. Fit the tiles closely together, leaving grouting gaps of no more than ⅛ in. (3mm) if you are laying ceramic. Fit spacers between the tiles, and hold the tiles down with short strips of painter's tape. Then fill in the spaces between the chalk lines, working from the center of the room toward the walls, until the whole floor apart from the edges is laid out in a dry run.

Step 2
Cut tiles to fit around the edges (☛ pages 26–27), allowing for a ⅛ in. (3mm) grouting gap along the wall. Use card or Kraft paper templates to help shape tiles around pipes, vents and corners (☛ page 27). Split ceramic tiles with a tile cutter or tile saw, and use the tile nippers for curves. Cut clay tiles with an angle grinder or diamond wheel cutter. Drill holes with a masonry bit, smoothing with a half-round file.

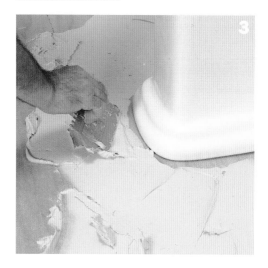

Step 3

Once the entire floor is covered, and you are happy with the overall effect, lift about 10 tiles in the corner furthest from the exit. Pour a little adhesive onto the floor and spread with a notched trowel (if you don't have one, you can use the plastic spreader supplied with the adhesive), combing slightly. Continue until the section is spread to a depth of around ¼ in. (6mm).

Step 5

Lift another section of about 10 tiles, and continue in the same way until you have worked your way across the floor. Do not spread more adhesive than you can cover in an hour, as it sets quickly. Try not to kneel or walk on newly laid tiles, and wipe off surplus adhesive with a damp cloth or sponge as you go.

Step 7

Grout the tiles, working with about 1 pint (0.5L) of grout at a time. Starting in a corner, pour grout into the gaps between the tiles, and use a grouting float to push it in evenly. Tilt the float at an angle of 60 degrees to the floor, pressing down firmly to ensure that the joints are completely filled, and work in a figure-eight motion over the tile joints so the grout is inserted evenly.

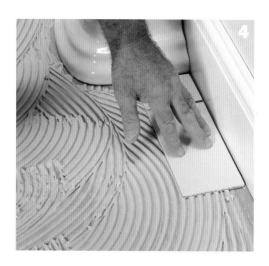

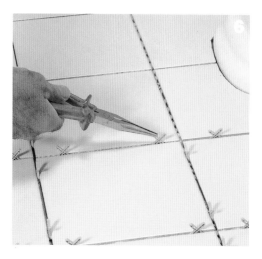

Step 4

Lay the tiles from the walls inward, working toward the exit. Fit spacers if required, as before, and twist each tile a little as you embed it in the adhesive, for a better bond. Tap each tile down with a rubber mallet to expel any air beneath. Monitor the floor level as you go, using a carpenter's level (rest it on a straightedge if necessary).

Step 6

Leave the tiles to set overnight and then remove any spacers, using pliers.

Step 8

Wipe excess grout off the surface of the tiles with a damp sponge as you go. Wipe each tile once only, working diagonally across the tile, so you don't pull grout out of the joints. Rinse the sponge in clean water as needed, wringing out so as not to add water to the grout mixture.

Step 9
When you've finished grouting and wiping the whole floor, go back to the beginning and smooth down the grout lines with a dowel or grouting tool. Leave the grout to dry for 3 hours.

Step 11 (Areas where water is used)
A ceramic or clay floor in a kitchen or bathroom must be waterproofed by sealing the gaps between the tiles and the walls and base of fixtures with caulking. Apply the caulking with a caulking gun, and avoid touching for 24 hours.

THE FLOORING LAYERS

Laying on a concrete subfloor

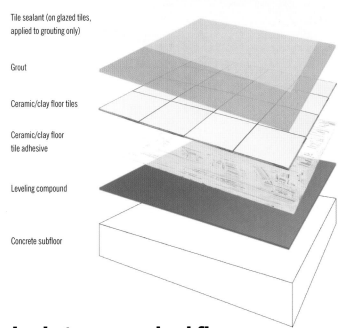

Tile sealant (on glazed tiles, applied to grouting only)

Grout

Ceramic/clay floor tiles

Ceramic/clay floor tile adhesive

Leveling compound

Concrete subfloor

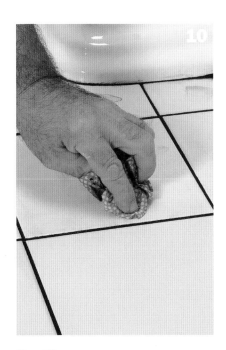

Step 10
Use water and a soft cloth or sponge to clean any smears of grout from the surface of the tiles.

Step 12
Vacuum or sweep the floor to remove any particles of dust or grit. Then seal the grout lines with tile sealant, working it well into the grout lines with a clean ½ in. (1.25cm) paintbrush. Try not to drop sealant on the tiles, and wipe off any excess immediately. Leave to dry for 4 hours. (If you are laying unglazed tiles, apply sealant to the whole floor using a paint roller. Mop up any excess sealant with a clean cloth 30 minutes after application, and leave to dry overnight.)

Laying on a wood subfloor

Tile sealant (on glazed tiles, applied to grouting only)

Grout

Ceramic/clay floor tiles

Ceramic/clay floor tile adhesive

¼ in. (6mm) marine plywood treated with diluted PVA adhesive

Existing joists and wood boards

Terra-cotta

PROPERTIES AT A GLANCE
(*low, **medium, ***high)
• HARD WEARING ***
• WATER RESISTANCE ***
• HEAT RETENTION **
• LOW MAINTENANCE **
• SOUND INSULATION *

Terra-cotta literally means "fired earth," and it is the warm earthy hue of this flooring that gives it its characteristic charm. Like clay and ceramic tiles, terra-cotta is manufactured from clay, but it is fired at a lower temperature. The process leaves air pockets within the tiles, which retain heat, making this the cosiest of the hard floors. The presence of air pockets also makes terra-cotta more porous than ceramic or clay and so, since the tiles are usually sold unsealed, repeated sealing is required during installation, as well as regular maintenance afterward. Softer than other hard tiles, terra-cotta soon becomes worn and pitted, but the rich patina of aged terra-cotta is part of its appeal—and the floor itself is very durable.

Terra-cotta is often laid with wide grout lines (up to ¾ in./2cm) to produce a rustic look. As a result this floor is relatively easy to install, as imperfections add to the charm, rather than disrupt a flawless effect. Less suitable for a formal setting, terra-cotta works very well in a kitchen, as long as the tiles are properly sealed. The warmth of terra-cotta would make it pleasant underfoot in a bathroom, but spilled water may be retained in the hollows of a pitted surface.

Designing the floor

Terra-cotta tiles come in attractive earth tones, from fiery orange to dusky pink to brick-red. Variations of heat during firing and the blending of different clays can create variegated tiles where colors blend softly into one another. New terra-cotta tiles are produced with a range of finishes, some smooth and others distressed with pockmarks. You can even buy antique terra-cotta tiles, which glow with the patina of age. Handmade tiles may vary more in tone and thickness than the cleaner-lined products of a machine (so make sure you harmonize variations in color or depth when laying out the floor). Although terra-cotta is usually sold unsealed, it is sometimes possible to buy tiles glazed in colors such as shiny blue or green.

Terra-cotta tiles are often installed in simple patterns, with the subtle differences in color and shade between individual tiles producing an inviting, natural floor. Alternatively, create a more dramatic design, making use of contrasting colors in a checkerboard layout, for example, or incorporating differently sized squares or shapes such as hexagons or diamonds. Terra-cotta tiles are relatively soft, so you could even cut them to suit your own unique design.

Below: Wide grout lines and an uneven, pitted floor surface create the look of a traditionally aged floor.

Maintenance

Terra-cotta tiles are porous and therefore should be treated regularly with a wax polish. Traditionally, terra-cotta is finished with coats of linseed oil and wax, but many easy-to-apply finishes and sealants are now available (ask your supplier for recommendations). Polish a new floor once a week for six weeks, then at six-week intervals. Apply the polish with a soft cloth or an electric polisher. You should also sweep the floor regularly or vacuum, taking care not to scratch the tiles. Clean off dirt with a wet mop, using diluted household detergent. Metal brushes can permanently mark the floor, so if you need to scrub, use a brush with nylon or natural bristles.

Advantages
- Durable.
- Water-resistant (if sealed properly).
- Warmer underfoot than other hard floors.
- Available in beautifully warm, soft shades.
- Particularly suitable for kitchens, hallways and country settings.

Disadvantages
- Requires regular maintenance to remain waterproof.

HEXAGONS

SQUARES

SQUARES AND RECTANGLES

Opposite: This floor of hexagonal terra-cotta tiles is reminiscent of cobblestones, lending a refreshingly unusual look to a traditional material.

Above: Variations in color and shape (here triangles, rectangles and different sizes of squares are used) add interest to a floor. Make sure that any variations in the tiles are balanced carefully across the floor as a whole.

Right: The traditional qualities of burnt-earth tiles are much sought after today; they have no pattern to wear out, only a patina of age to gain.

Laying a terra-cotta floor

LEVEL OF DIFFICULTY
●●●○○

Terra-cotta tiles are often laid loosely spaced, a look that allows for some mistakes during installation. They are harder to cut than ceramic tiles, however, and very porous, which means that they will need to be properly sealed and maintained.

Before you begin laying your terra-cotta floor, remove existing floor coverings, and ensure that the subfloor is clean and smooth. Level concrete floors with leveling compound and cover wood floorboards with ¼ in. (6mm) marine plywood treated with diluted PVA adhesive (☞ pages 18–21). Make a floor plan to calculate how many tiles you need, and map out any pattern to ensure an even layout (☞ pages 12–15). For terra-cotta floors a more rustic look is generally desired, with grouting gaps of up to ¾ in. (2cm), so tile spacers are not usually needed. If you want to lay a more closely jointed floor, however, insert spacers between the tiles when they are laid out and remove them before grouting.

Golden rules
- Prepare the site before starting (☞ pages 18–21).
- Buy all materials at the same time to guarantee consistency and availability.
- Ask your supplier for advice and follow the manufacturer's instructions.
- Work safely. Ventilate the room well, and wear strong rubber gloves when working with adhesive, sealant, grout or caulking. Wear a mask, safety glasses, gloves and ear protection when using power tools, and ensure that tiles to be cut are secured firmly.

Toolbox
1. 2 IN. (5CM) PAINTBRUSH
2. CHALK LINE
3. PAINTER'S TAPE
4. TILE SPACERS (OPTIONAL)
5. ANGLE GRINDER
6. MASONRY BIT
   AND HALF-ROUND FILE
7. ⅛ IN. (3MM)
   NOTCHED TROWEL
8. RUBBER MALLET
9. CARPENTER'S LEVEL
10. STRAIGHTEDGE
11. CLEAN CLOTHS/SPONGES
12. VACUUM CLEANER/
    SOFT BRUSH OR BROOM
13. PAINT ROLLER
14. GROUTING FLOAT
15. DOWEL/GROUTING TOOL
16. CAULKING GUN (FOR
    WET AREAS)
17. ELECTRIC POLISHER
    (OPTIONAL)

Materials
18. TERRA-COTTA TILES
19. TERRA-COTTA
    TILE SEALANT
20. CARD/KRAFT PAPER
21. TERRA-COTTA
    TILE ADHESIVE
22. GROUT
23. CAULKING (FOR
    WET AREAS)
24. TERRA-COTTA WAX POLISH

INSTALLING TERRA-COTTA TILES

Preparing the tiles

Terra-cotta is a very porous material and can become stained by adhesive or grout. Turn all tiles face up (some terra-cotta tiles may be laid with either side up, so choose which side is to face up now), wipe off any dust with a slightly damp cloth, and paint the top side of the tiles with a coat of terra-cotta tile sealant, using a paintbrush. Mop up excess sealant with a clean cloth 30 minutes after application, and leave to dry overnight. Avoid putting pressure on the tiles while the sealant is drying.

Sort the tiles to ensure that variations in tone or thickness are evenly distributed, and stack them in piles, with tiles laid top side up, placed conveniently around the room. Terra-cotta tiles are prone to chipping, so put aside marked tiles to cut for the perimeter.

Mark two chalk lines at right angles across the center of the room, to act as guides in laying out the floor, and adjust them according to the quarter method (☞ page 14).

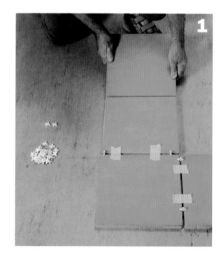

Step 1
Lay out the tiles without adhesive along the adjusted chalk lines. Use short strips of painter's tape, if necessary, to prevent the tiles from moving as you work. Leave grouting spaces between the tiles of up to ¾ in. (2cm), depending on the look you want to achieve (use tile spacers to achieve a more precise installation). Then fill in the quarters of the room, working from the center of the room toward the walls, until the whole floor, except the edges, is laid out in a dry run.

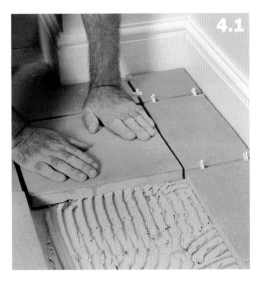

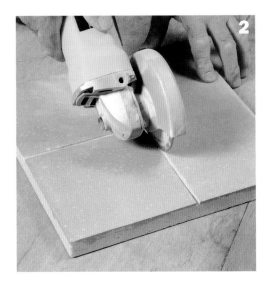

Step 2

Cut edge tiles to fit (☞ pages 26–27), allowing for a grouting gap of at least ⅛ in. (3mm) along the walls (a full ¾ in./2cm is probably too wide here). Use card or Kraft paper templates to shape tiles around pipes, vents and corners (☞ page 27). Cut tiles with an angle grinder, or, if thin enough, snap them with a tile scorer, cold chisel and hammer. Drill holes with a masonry bit, and smooth with a half-round file.

Step 4

Lay the tiles from the walls inward, working toward the exit. Twist each tile a little as you embed it in the adhesive for a better bond, and remember to fit spacers, if required. Tap each tile down with a rubber mallet to expel any air beneath. Monitor the floor level as you go, using a carpenter's level (rest it on a straightedge if necessary).

Step 3

When the floor is completely covered, and you are happy with the overall effect, lift about 10 tiles in the corner furthest from the exit. Pour a little adhesive onto the floor and spread with a notched trowel, combing slightly. Continue until the exposed area is spread to a depth of about ¼ in. (6mm).

Step 5

Lift another section of about 10 tiles and continue in the same way until you have worked across the floor. Do not spread more adhesive than you can cover in an hour, as it sets quickly. Try not to kneel or walk on newly laid tiles, and wipe off surplus adhesive with a damp cloth or sponge as you go. Leave the tiles to set overnight.

Step 6
Remove any spacers. Sweep or vacuum thoroughly to pick up any loose particles, and then paint a second coat of sealant over the tiles using a paint roller. Mop up excess sealant with a clean cloth 30 minutes after application, and leave to dry overnight.

Step 7
Grout the tiles, working with about 1 pint (0.5L) of grout at a time. Starting in a corner, pour grout into the gaps between the tiles, and use a grouting float to push it in evenly. Tilt the float at an angle of 60 degrees to the floor, and press down firmly to ensure that the joints are completely filled.

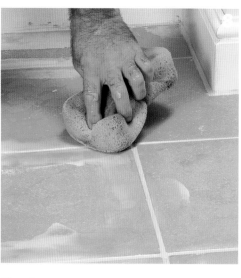

Step 8
Wipe excess grout off the surface of the tiles with a damp sponge as you go. Wipe each tile once only, working diagonally across the tile, so you don't pull grout out of the joints. Rinse the sponge in clean water as needed, wringing well.

Step 9
When you've finished grouting and wiping the whole floor, go back to the beginning and smooth down the grout lines with a dowel or grouting tool. Leave the grout to set for 3 hours.

Step 10
Use water and a soft cloth to clean any smears of grout from the surface of the tiles.

Step 11 (Areas where water is used)
A terra-cotta floor in a kitchen, bathroom or other area where water is used must be waterproofed by sealing the gaps between the tiles and the walls and base of fixtures with caulking. Apply the caulking with a caulking gun and leave to dry for 24 hours.

Step 12
Vacuum the floor, or sweep thoroughly with a soft broom, to remove any particles of dust or grit. Then seal the surface of the tiles for a third time, using the paint roller. Don't forget to work the sealant well into the grout lines. Mop up any excess sealant with a clean cloth 30 minutes after application, and leave to dry overnight.

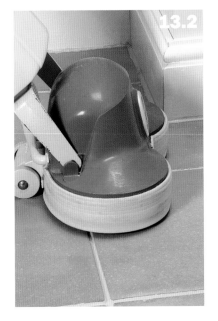

Step 13
Apply a coat of terra-cotta wax polish, and buff the surface using a soft cloth or electric polisher. Terra-cotta is very porous and reapplications of wax polish will be required to keep the floor waterproof (☛ page 35 for more information on maintenance).

THE FLOORING LAYERS

Laying on a concrete subfloor

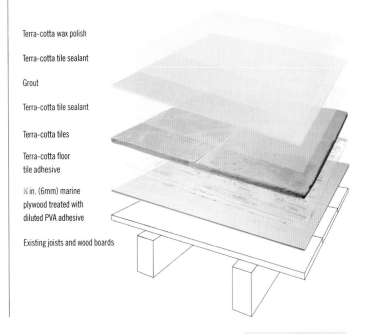

Terra-cotta wax polish

Terra-cotta tile sealant

Grout

Terra-cotta tile sealant

Terra-cotta tiles

Terra-cotta floor tile adhesive

Leveling compound

Concrete subfloor

Laying on a wood subfloor

Terra-cotta wax polish

Terra-cotta tile sealant

Grout

Terra-cotta tile sealant

Terra-cotta tiles

Terra-cotta floor tile adhesive

¼ in. (6mm) marine plywood treated with diluted PVA adhesive

Existing joists and wood boards

Mosaic

PROPERTIES AT A GLANCE
(*low, **medium, ***high)
• WATER RESISTANCE ***
• HARD WEARING **
• LOW MAINTENANCE **
• HEAT RETENTION *
• SOUND INSULATION *

Few floorings have as much character as mosaic. The basis of mosaic work is the combination of tiny colored tiles, called "tesserae," to achieve a floor that may be plain, or feature a geometrical or even pictorial design. At its most delicate, mosaic is almost like painting, using small blocks of color instead of brushwork, but assembling tesserae piece by piece into a complicated design is a painstaking and skilled task that is beyond the scope of most amateur floorlayers (although small sections might be attempted). A much easier and faster alternative is to buy mosaic tiles composed of tesserae attached to a scrim backing, which can be easily glued to the floor, and cut to size with shears or scissors if necessary. Mosaic is less durable than other hard tiles and many resilient floorings, so is chosen less for its long life than its creative possibilities and characteristically segmented appearance.

Mosaic can be overwhelming over a large expanse, and its intricacy often works best in small areas (which are also easier to deal with if you want to cut up the scrim-backed tiles to create your own pattern). Tesserae are usually glazed ceramic and are therefore water-resistant (be sure to seal any unglazed tiles with the recommended sealant), so the bathroom is a popular location—as indeed it was in Roman times. Mosaic

GUILLOCHE BORDER

GREEK KEY BORDER

Designing the floor

The tesserae of mosaic tiles are usually ceramic, glazed with a matte or gloss finish. Tiles come in a range of colors, including earth tones—you can buy mosaic tiles that resemble pebbles for an outdoors feel in a bathroom—as well as jewel-like shades of red, blue and green, and of course simple black or white. The easiest floor for an amateur to achieve is single color, using tiles of one shade only, perhaps with a contrasting grout to emphasize the segmentation of the flooring. Combining one or two colors of tile can produce simple but effective geometric designs, and this can be easily plotted on graph paper before you begin. If you want to be more adventurous, buy a range of colored tiles and cut the tesserae from the scrim backing to arrange them as you wish. Again, use graph paper to plot the design. You can even mix in different materials, such as glass or marble tesserae, which are available at specialist tile suppliers. It's best to start with simple, geometric designs, using ceramic tesserae of a consistent thickness.

If you are after true opulence, commission a mosaic artist to design and install the floor. This will be extremely expensive, but the result will be a work of art under your feet!

SCROLL BORDER

Above: For ease of installation, these days mosaic is usually sold in tiles composed of many individual tesserae attached to a scrim backing.

Right: Repeat patterns can be used over a large area to create a complex-looking design. Be sure to plan the layout carefully first to fit the available space.

Far right: A striking design can be built up using just a few colors. Start with a simple design, and plot it on graph paper before you begin.

also works well for a spectacular hallway, and can be very effective as a contrasting feature strip in any room.

Maintenance

Sweep regularly or vacuum, and clean off dirt with a wet mop, using diluted household detergent. Metal brushes can permanently mark the floor, so if you need to scrub, use a brush with nylon or natural bristles. Glazed tiles do not require sealing (although the grouting will), but your supplier will be able to offer various products to achieve a glossy finish—reapply coats as recommended and do not overpolish or the floor will become dangerously slippery.

Advantages
- Water-resistant.
- Very easy to cut.
- Produces a bright, lively effect, and offers great potential for creativity.
- Particularly suitable for bathrooms and hallways, and as a feature elsewhere.

Disadvantages
- Less durable than other hard tiles.
- Too much mosaic in a room can be overbearing.

Left: Some mosaic work is extremely delicate, creating the impression of fine brushstrokes and matching the opulence of floors from Roman times.

Right: Simple but effective: two complementary colors can produce a strong pattern across the floor as a whole.

Above: Use antique stone tesserae to create a beautifully aged mosaic floor in an instant.

Laying a mosaic floor

LEVEL OF DIFFICULTY

●●○○○

Mosaic tiles are easy to work with as they are light, can be cut to size easily and fit neatly together. Mosaic tiles are almost always glazed, so you will probably not need to seal them yourself. Very complex mosaic designs are, however, difficult to create—so start with something simple.

Toolbox

1 SHEARS/UTILITY KNIFE
2 TILE NIPPERS
3 CHALK LINE
4 TILE SPACERS (OPTIONAL)
5 PAINTER'S TAPE
6 ⅛ IN. (3MM) NOTCHED TROWEL
7 CARPENTER'S LEVEL
8 STRAIGHTEDGE
9 RUBBER MALLET
10 CLEAN SPONGES/CLOTHS
11 GROUTING FLOAT
12 CAULKING GUN (FOR WET AREAS)
13 VACUUM CLEANER/SOFT BRUSH OR BROOM
14 PAINT ROLLER (FOR UNGLAZED TILES ONLY)

Materials

15 MOSAIC TILES
16 CARD/KRAFT PAPER
17 MOSAIC FLOOR TILE ADHESIVE
18 WATERPROOF GROUT
19 CAULKING (FOR WET AREAS)
20 TILE SEALANT (FOR UNGLAZED TILES ONLY)

Before you begin laying your mosaic floor, remove existing floor coverings, and ensure that the subfloor is clean and smooth. Level concrete floors with leveling compound; cover wood floorboards with ¼ in. (6mm) marine plywood treated with diluted PVA adhesive (☛ pages 18–21 for detailed instructions). Make a floor plan to calculate how many tiles you need, and map out any design to ensure an accurate layout (☛ pages 12–15). Mosaic tiles are "self-spacing," and butting them up creates a grout line that matches the joints between individual tesserae. You may, however, want wider joints between tiles, in which case you can use plastic or homemade spacers to ensure consistent gaps.

Golden rules

- Prepare the site before starting (☛ pages 18–21), taking special care to ensure that the subfloor is rigid and level.
- Buy all materials at the same time to guarantee consistency and availability.
- Ask your supplier for advice and follow the manufacturer's instructions.
- Work safely. Ventilate the room well, and wear strong rubber gloves when working with adhesive, sealant, grout or caulking.

INSTALLING MOSAIC TILES

Preparing the tiles

If your design plan demands it, cut through the scrim backing to reduce the size of tiles as required. The scrim can be easily cut with shears or a utility knife; use tile nippers if you need to split one of the tiles attached to the scrim (to make a point on a star, for example). When you are ready, stack the tiles in convenient piles. Mark two chalk lines at right angles across the center of the room, to act as guides in laying out the floor, and adjust them according to the quarter method (☛ page 14). If you would like a border of contrasting tiles, start by laying this out first (☛ page 15).

Step 1

Lay the tiles dry along the adjusted chalk lines. Butting the scrim edges of the tiles close together will automatically produce the correct grouting space (insert spacers if a wider joint is required). Hold the tiles in place with short strips of painter's tape. Then fill in the spaces between the chalk lines, working from the center of the room toward the walls, until the whole floor, except the edges, is laid out in a dry run.

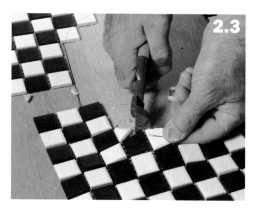

Step 2

Use card or Kraft paper templates to help fit tiles around pipes, vents and other obstacles (☞ page 27). Cut tiles with shears or a utility knife to fit around the edges, remembering to allow for a ⅛ in. (3mm) grouting gap along the walls. Snip tiles away from the scrim as required.

Step 3

Once the entire floor is covered, and you are happy with the overall effect, lift about 10 tiles in the corner furthest from the exit. Pour a little adhesive onto the floor and spread with a notched trowel, combing slightly. Continue until the exposed section is spread to a depth of around ¼ in. (6mm).

Step 4

Lay the tiles from the walls inward, working toward the exit. Twist each tile a little as you embed it in the adhesive for a better bond. Monitor the floor level as you go, using a carpenter's level (rest it on a straightedge if necessary).

Step 5

Lift another section of 10 tiles and continue in the same way until you have worked your way across the floor. Tap the tiles with a rubber mallet to expel any air beneath. Do not spread more adhesive than you can cover in an hour, as it sets quickly. Try not to kneel or walk on newly laid tiles, and wipe off surplus adhesive with a damp cloth or sponge as you go. Leave the floor to set overnight.

Step 6

Now grout the tiles, working with about 1 pint (0.5L) of grout at a time. (It is essential to use waterproof grout, as there are too many grout lines to seal.) Starting in the corner furthest from the exit, pour grout over the floor and use a grouting float to push it evenly into the joints. Tilt the float at a 60-degree angle to the floor, pressing down firmly to ensure that the joints are completely filled, and work in a figure-eight motion so that the grout is inserted evenly.

Step 7
Wipe excess grout off the surface of the tiles with a damp sponge as you go. Wipe each tile once only, working diagonally across the tile, so you don't pull grout out of the joints. Rinse the sponge in clean water as needed, wringing well.

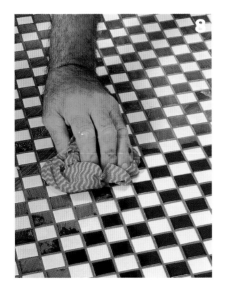

Step 8
Use a soft damp cloth to remove any remaining smears of grout from the surface of the tiles.

Step 9 (Areas where water is used)
A mosaic floor in a kitchen, bathroom or other room where water is used must be waterproofed by sealing the gaps between the tiles and the walls and base of fixtures with caulking. Apply the caulking with a caulking gun and leave to dry for 24 hours.

Step 10
There are too many grout lines on a mosaic floor to seal individually. Seal the whole floor only if you are using unglazed mosaic. In that case, sweep or vacuum up any particles of dust or grit, and apply a coat of tile sealant using a paint roller. Mop up any excess with a clean cloth 30 minutes after application, and leave to dry overnight.

THE FLOORING LAYERS

Laying on a concrete subfloor

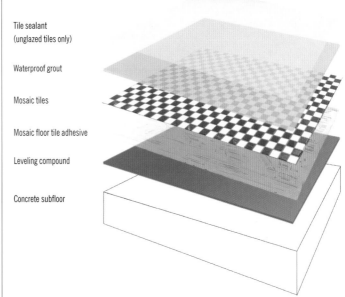

Tile sealant (unglazed tiles only)

Waterproof grout

Mosaic tiles

Mosaic floor tile adhesive

Leveling compound

Concrete subfloor

Laying on a wood subfloor

Tile sealant (unglazed tiles only)

Waterproof grout

Mosaic tiles

Mosaic floor tile adhesive

¼ in. (6mm) marine plywood treated with diluted PVA adhesive

Existing joists and wood boards

Slate

PROPERTIES AT A GLANCE
(*low, **medium, ***high)
- HARD WEARING ***
- LOW MAINTENANCE ***
- WATER RESISTANCE ***
- HEAT RETENTION *
- SOUND INSULATION *

A natural rock, slate is extremely durable, requires little maintenance, hides dirt well and has a tendency to split perfectly along a plane to produce thin, tough sheets—making it an ideal material for flooring. It also creates a dramatic décor, and offers intriguing variations of color and pattern in every tile. Natural stone of this quality isn't cheap, but it is less expensive than marble or granite, and unlike these can be installed by a nonprofessional.

Slate is supplied as riven (split) slates or as cut tiles. A riven surface is slightly rough and provides some slip resistance. Riven slates are uneven in thickness, so take this into account when installing them (start with the thickest slates and use adhesive to build up the thinner ones). Cut tiles have a smooth surface with precise edges, but may be slippery—take care not to polish them too highly.

Most slate is waterproof, so is suitable for areas where moisture may be an issue, such as basements or semi-outdoor sites like verandahs. Rugged, durable and easy to clean, slate is also ideal for kitchens. Being so tough, slate is supplied in thinner tiles than stone, which makes it a possible choice for an

MOLE RIVEN

MOLE HONED

Designing the floor

Don't assume that slate has to be black or gray. This stone comes in a wide variety of light and dark shades, including beiges, reds, rusts, blues, purples and browns. You can buy single-color slate and also wonderful naturally multicolored tiles with shades such as orange, red and gold over a dark background.

Source neatly cut square tiles for a nearly groutless, perfectly aligned look in a contemporary setting, or set irregularly shaped tiles in wide grout lines for a more old-fashioned or country cottage effect. Slate tiles are square, rectangular, octagonal or randomly cut (for a "crazy paving" look), and come in various sizes, from large flagstone to paver to inset tile.

Slate has a naturally wet sheen, and this can be enhanced by finishing products. You can polish the floor to the gloss of your choice, but take care not to make it too slippery. Riven slate tends to have a rough finish, while cut tiles are smoother to the touch.

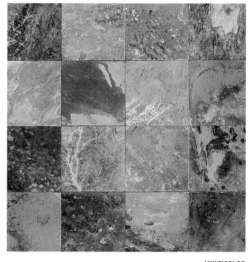

MULTICOLOR

EARTH

RUST

BLACK

SILVER BLUE

BRONZES AND GRAYS

BLACKS

upstairs bathroom (though it is still heavy—check that the subfloor can take the weight). Choose a textured variety of slate for a bathroom to avoid a slippery floor.

Maintenance

Sweep regularly or vacuum, and clean off dirt with a wet mop, using diluted household detergent. Metal brushes can permanently mark the floor, so if you need to scrub, use a brush with nylon or natural bristles. Slate is usually waterproof and does not require sealing, but you may want to apply a finish to give the floor extra luster. Treat the tiles to a further coat of product every 6 to 12 months to maintain the shine.

Advantages
- Extremely durable.
- Easy to maintain.
- Water-resistant.
- Beautiful, subtle colors and textures.
- Ideal for kitchens, hallways and porches.

Disadvantages
- Expensive.
- Cold and hard.
- Can be slippery.

Left: Don't feel that your choice of color is confined to gray or black. Shades of beige slate will bring warmth to a floor.

Left: Slate is a popular choice for hallways, since it is water-resistant, easy to clean and provides an impressive entrance into the home.

Right: For a contemporary look choose perfectly aligned squares with narrow grout lines.

Left: An interesting variation on the traditional checkerboard layout is to stagger the joints between tiles so that they fall at the mid-point of tiles in the adjacent rows instead of lining up across the rows.

Above: Slate can be marvelously variegated, with the same tile colored with shades of beige, orange and blue-black.

Laying a slate floor

LEVEL OF DIFFICULTY

●●●○○

Varying thicknesses, a tendency to fracture and the sharpness of the shards make slate an awkward floor to lay. Slate tiles are usually waterproof, however, so you will only need to seal the grout lines.

Toolbox

1 CHALK LINE
2 TILE SPACERS (OPTIONAL)
3 ANGLE GRINDER
4 MASONRY BIT
AND HALF-ROUND FILE
5 ⅛ IN. (3MM)
NOTCHED TROWEL
6 RUBBER MALLET
7 CARPENTER'S LEVEL
8 STRAIGHTEDGE
9 CLEAN SPONGES/CLOTHS
10 GROUTING FLOAT
11 DOWEL/GROUTING TOOL
12 CAULKING GUN (FOR
WET AREAS)
13 VACUUM CLEANER/SOFT
BRUSH OR BROOM
14 ½ IN. (1.25CM) PAINTBRUSH

Materials

15 SLATE TILES
16 KRAFT PAPER/CARD
17 SLATE FLOOR
TILE ADHESIVE
18 GROUT
19 CAULKING (FOR
WET AREAS)
20 TILE SEALANT

Before you begin laying your slate floor, remove any existing floor coverings (slate can be laid over old tiles so long as they are well stuck down, but this may raise the height of the floor unacceptably), and ensure the subfloor is clean and smooth. Level concrete floors with leveling compound and cover wood floorboards with ¼ in. (6mm) marine plywood treated with diluted PVA adhesive (☞ pages 18–21). Make a floor plan to calculate how many tiles you need, and map out any pattern to ensure an even layout (☞ pages 12–15). When laying out the floor, you can use tile spacers to ensure consistent joints. X-shaped spacers are easier to remove if fitted "standing up"; alternatively, cut pieces of plywood or strips of packaging to a suitable length.

Golden rules

- Prepare the site before starting (☞ pages 18–21).
- Buy all materials at the same time to guarantee consistency and availability.
- Ask your supplier for advice and follow the manufacturer's instructions.
- Work safely. Long gloves that cover your wrists will help to protect you from sharp slate edges. Ventilate the room well, and wear strong rubber gloves when working with adhesive, sealant, grout or caulking. Wear a mask, safety glasses, gloves and ear protection when using power tools, and ensure that tiles to be cut are secured firmly.

INSTALLING SLATE TILES

Preparing the tiles

Slate is sharper than most flooring materials, so take care. Slate tiles can vary in thickness, and you will need to sort them accordingly before laying out the floor. You'll be able to use all the tiles, but you may need to adjust the amount of adhesive you apply by a fraction in order to keep the floor level. Slate is prone to chipping, so put aside any damaged tiles to cut for edge pieces. Also sort the tiles for any variation in color, and stack them in piles placed conveniently around the room. Then mark two chalk lines at right angles across the center of the room, to act as guides in laying out the floor, and adjust them according to the quarter method (☞ page 14).

USEFUL TIP
There may be variation in the grain and color as well as the thickness of slates. Watch out for dramatically different slates that might stand out too much.

USEFUL TIP
Keep the floor level by laying the thicker slates first and using extra adhesive to build up the thinner tiles.

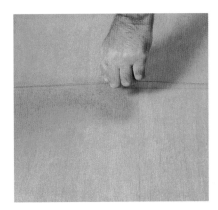

Step 1
Lay tiles dry along the adjusted chalk lines. Leave spaces of about ¼ or ½ in. (6mm or 1.25cm) between the tiles for grouting (use tile spacers if necessary). Then fill in the spaces between the chalk lines, working from the center of the room toward the walls until the whole floor, apart from the edges, is laid out in a dry run.

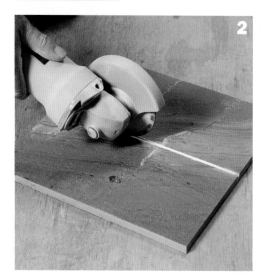

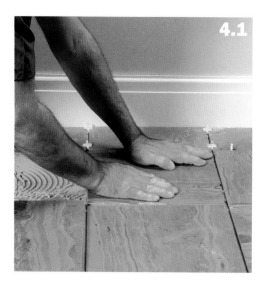

Step 2

Cut tiles to fit around the room's edges (☞ pages 26–27), remembering to allow for a ⅛ in. (3mm) grouting gap along the walls. Cut tiles with an angle grinder (you may be able to snap thinner slates with a tile scorer, cold chisel and hammer). Drill holes with a masonry bit, smoothing with a half-round file. Use card or Kraft paper templates to help shape tiles around pipes, vents and corners (☞ page 27).

Step 5

Lift another section of about 10 tiles and continue in the same way until you have worked your way across the floor. Do not spread more adhesive than you can cover in an hour, as it sets quickly. Try not to kneel or walk on newly laid tiles, and wipe off surplus adhesive with a damp cloth or sponge as you go. Leave the tiles to set overnight.

Step 4

Lay the tiles from the walls inward, working toward the exit. Fit spacers if required, and twist each tile a little as you embed it for a better bond. Tap each tile down with a rubber mallet to expel the air beneath. Monitor the floor level as you go, using a carpenter's level (rest it on a straightedge if necessary), and use more adhesive to make up for thinner slates.

Step 3

Once the entire floor is covered, and you are happy with the overall effect, lift about 10 slates in the corner of the room furthest from the exit. Pour a little adhesive onto the floor and spread with a notched trowel, combing slightly. Continue until the exposed section is spread to a depth of about ¼ in. (6mm).

Step 6

Remove any spacers and grout the tiles, working with about 1 pint (0.5L) of grout at a time. Starting in a corner, pour grout into the joints, pushing it in evenly with a grouting float. Tilt the float at an angle of 60 degrees to the floor, pressing down firmly to ensure that the joints are completely filled.

THE FLOORING LAYERS

Laying on a concrete subfloor

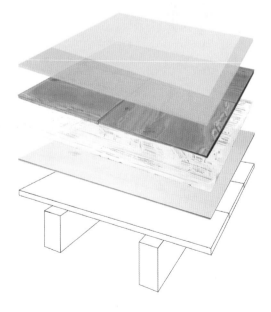

Tile sealant (applied to grout lines only)

Grout

Slate tiles

Slate floor tile adhesive

Leveling compound

Concrete subfloor

Laying on a wood subfloor

Tile sealant (applied to grout lines only)

Grout

Slate tiles

Slate floor tile adhesive

¼ in. (6mm) marine plywood treated with diluted PVA adhesive

Existing joists and wood boards

Step 7
Wipe excess grout off the surface of the tiles with a damp sponge as you go. Wipe each tile once only, working diagonally across the tile, so you don't pull grout out of the joints. Rinse the sponge in clean water as needed, wringing to remove excess water. When you've finished grouting and wiping the whole floor, go back to the beginning and smooth down the grout lines with a dowel or grouting tool. Leave the grout to dry for 3 hours.

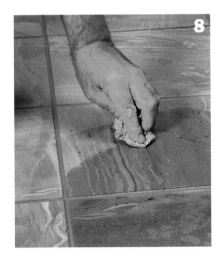

Step 8
Use water and a soft cloth to clean any smears of grout from the surface of the tiles.

Step 9 (Areas where water is used)
A slate floor in a kitchen, bathroom or other area where water is used must be waterproofed by sealing the gaps between the tiles and the walls with caulking. Apply the caulking with a caulking gun and leave to dry for 24 hours.

Step 10
Vacuum or sweep up any particles of dust or grit. Then seal the grout lines with tile sealant, working it well into the grout lines with a clean ½ in. (1.25cm) paintbrush. Try not to drop sealant on the tiles, and wipe off any excess immediately. Leave to dry for 4 hours.

Limestone and sandstone

PROPERTIES AT A GLANCE
(*low, **medium, ***high)
• HARD WEARING ***
• LOW MAINTENANCE ***
• WATER RESISTANCE ***
• HEAT RETENTION *
• SOUND INSULATION *

A limestone or sandstone floor could last for a thousand years, so it's reassuring to know that their subtle tones provide a superb backdrop to any number of interior decoration schemes. Perhaps the most versatile of the natural stone floors, these tiles are available in a range of beautifully neutral shades that will sit happily with any change of furnishing. And you can still pick the floor that suits the style of architecture of your home: there are enough different looks to match every setting, whether you live in an elegant home or a country cottage.

The visual effect of a stone floor will often warm a room, but it will usually feel hard and cold underfoot—so consider installing underfloor heating. Sandstone in particular can be rough to walk on, but avoid very smooth tiles in potentially wet areas, such as a kitchen or bathroom, as the floor may become dangerously slippery. Apply a nonslip, matte finish to floors in these sites. The tiles are waterproof when sealed, but if you omit this step the stone will stain.

Limestone and sandstone are available as slabs and tiles. Slabs are usually laid by professionals: they are very difficult to handle and must be precut to the exact dimensions of your home. Tiles are also heavy, however, so take that into account when choosing the flooring. You should really only lay stone on a concrete subfloor—if you are considering installing on a wood subfloor ask a builder to check that it can take the weight of the

Designing the floor

BLUE LIMESTONE

BUFF SANDSTONE

Sandstone usually comes in attractive pale shades of cream, yellow, pink and red, while limestone offers a wider range of colors, including white, gray, brown-red, green-blue and near black. Travertine is a distinctive light yellowish limestone found near springs. Natural impurities in both rocks provide subtle variations in tone across the tiles. Limestone may even display a cross-section of fossils such as corals, sea-lilies and shellfish; these work very well as feature strips among plainer tiles.

GOLD LIMESTONE

ROSE SANDSTONE

Limestone and sandstone offer a variety of looks to suit every setting. Simply seal the tiles for a matte effect, or polish them to the sheen of your choice (taking care not to make the floor too slippery). One popular effect is to lay rectangular tiles in a random style, with staggered joints, to mimic the rustic feel of an old farmhouse. Alternatively, you can choose smooth octagonal tiles, and small diamond inset tiles in a contrasting or complementary color, for a more formal look. Close-set stone tiles, perhaps in different sizes, give a disciplined, modular feel to a floor, and you can choose whether you want visible, contrasting grout lines or a nearly seamless look. You could also use irregular stones—"crazy paving"—but take care to avoid a confused effect.

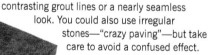

FINISHES

COMPLEMENTARY SHADES OF LIMESTONE

SANDSTONE PARQUET

tiles. Stone is not easy to install: a rustic, country effect allows some room for irregularities, but a formal, stone floor must be laid perfectly, as any mistakes in the grout lines or any surface unevenness will be prominent.

Maintenance

Sweep regularly or vacuum, and clean off dirt with a wet mop, using diluted household detergent. Metal brushes can permanently mark the floor, so if you need to scrub, use a brush with nylon or natural bristles. Various finishes are available to achieve the desired gloss or matte effect. Treat the floor with a further coat of sealant every 6 to 12 months.

Advantages
- Extremely durable.
- Easy to maintain.
- A versatile floor that suits many settings.
- Particularly suitable for kitchens, formal living areas and hallways.

Disadvantages
- Hard underfoot.
- Expensive.
- Usually too heavy for upper stories.
- Can be difficult to lay.

Left: This floor has been polished to highlight the many tones of matte-black, blue-gray and beige-brown that characterize this Indian limestone.

Above: There are so many different shades of limestone and sandstone that you can choose a color to suit your décor. Here, white limestone complements furniture and walls, lending a sense of Zen-like calm to the room.

Top left: Huge pale limestone tiles, with nearly invisible grouting, bring an airy elegance to the setting.

Above: Easy to clean and maintain, a precisely aligned limestone floor is both a practical and an attractive choice for a contemporary kitchen.

Top right: Travertine is a distinctive light honey-yellow limestone. Choose a pale stone if you want to warm up your décor.

Above: Rosy stone tiles provide a simple backing for ornate inset tiles and a complex border, producing a floor that is decorative without being fussy.

Laying a limestone or sandstone floor

LEVEL OF DIFFICULTY

●●●●○

Heavy and often large stone slabs or flags are awkward to handle. Limestone and sandstone are porous, so you will need to seal them to prevent staining. Mortar is more difficult to work with than adhesive, as it sets faster.

These heavy, bulky tiles are laid with mortar, which provides a stronger bond than adhesive, and are usually installed on a concrete subfloor. If you want to lay limestone or sandstone on wood, check that the subfloor can take the load. You must cover a wood subfloor with polyethylene sheet or liquid damp-proof membrane to prevent the wood from wicking water from the mortar as it dries, which may weaken the mortar and rot the wood. You do not need to apply levelling compound to a concrete subfloor, or level boards with marine plywood, unless the subfloor is very uneven, as the mortar bed will smooth out irregularities (☛ page 18–21 for detailed instructions on preparing the site). Make a floor plan to calculate how many tiles you need, and map out any pattern to ensure an even layout (☛ pages 12–15). These heavy stones do not readily move out of place, but using spacers will help you achieve consistent grout lines on a narrowly jointed floor. Longer spacers are easier to remove: you can make your own from pieces of plywood or packaging cut to the required length.

Golden rules

- Check the subfloor can take the load of tiles and mortar.
- Prepare the site before starting (☛ pages 18–21).
- Ask your supplier for advice and follow the manufacturer's instructions.
- Work safely. Ventilate the room well, and wear strong rubber gloves when working with mortar, sealant, grout or caulking. Wear a mask, safety glasses, gloves and ear protection when using power tools, and ensure that tiles to be cut are secured firmly.

Toolbox

1 CHALK LINE
2 TILE SPACERS (OPTIONAL)
3 ANGLE GRINDER
4 MASONRY BIT AND HALF-ROUND FILE
5 DIAMOND WHEEL CUTTER
6 VACUUM CLEANER/SOFT BROOM OR BRUSH
7 PAINT ROLLER
8 WHISK
9 MASON'S TROWEL
10 RUBBER MALLET
11 SPIRIT-LEVEL
12 STRAIGHTEDGE
13 CLEAN SPONGES/CLOTHS
14 POINTING TROWEL
15 DOWEL/GROUTING TOOL
16 CAULKING GUN (FOR WET AREAS ONLY)

Materials

17 STONE TILES
18 CARD/PAPER
19 STONE TILE SEALANT
20 MORTAR MIX
21 CAULKING (FOR WET AREAS ONLY)

INSTALLING LIMESTONE AND SANDSTONE TILES

Preparing the tiles

Sort the tiles for tonal variations, and stack them in piles placed conveniently around the room. If you are using old, irregular stone tiles, plan the layout so that the largest flags are near the centre of the room, and the smaller ones around the edges (this also entails less cutting). Stone slabs can be very heavy, so take great care when carrying and stacking them. Before you start, mark two chalk lines at right angles across the centre of the room, to act as guides in laying out the floor, and adjust them according to the quarter method (☛ page 14).

USEFUL TIP
Sandstone and limestone tiles are bulky and should be laid with joints of at least 3–6mm (⅛–¼ in.) to allow for sufficient grouting to hold the tiles in place.

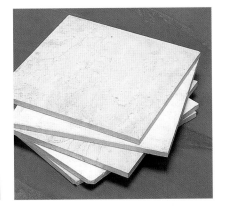

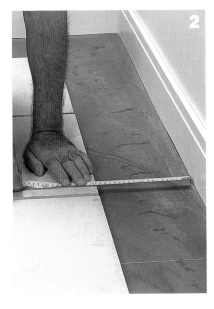

Step 1
Lay the tiles dry along the adjusted chalk lines. Leave 3mm–2cm (⅛–¾ in.) for grouting, depending on whether you want a very tight finish or a more irregular rustic look (use spacers if necessary). Fill in the spaces between the chalk lines, working from the centre of the room towards the walls, until the whole floor, except the edges, is laid out in a dry run.

Step 2
Measure the gaps at the edges to calculate the width of the edge tiles. Remember to subtract at least 6mm (¼ in.) from the measurement to allow for grouting gaps between the tiles and at the wall (2 x 3mm/⅛ in.).

Step 3

Cut the edge tiles to fit (pages 26–27), using card or Kraft paper templates to help shape them around pipes, vents and corners. Split tiles and cut curves with an angle grinder. Drill holes with a masonry bit, smoothing with a half-round file. A diamond wheel cutter is useful for cutting large quantities of tiles.

Step 5

Once the entire floor is laid out, and you are happy with the overall effect, mix up a quantity of mortar with a whisk or trowel. Stir water into the mortar mix (available premixed from building suppliers) until you achieve a creamy consistency. Mortar sets quickly in the bucket so mix up no more than you can use in an hour—start with a half-bucketful.

Step 8

Lift another section of about 10 tiles and continue in the same way until you have worked your way across the floor. Try not to kneel or walk on newly laid tiles, and wipe off surplus mortar with a damp sponge or cloth as you go. Leave to set for at least 3 hours.

Step 4

Before adhering the tiles, remove any particles of dust or grit with a soft broom or vacuum cleaner. Seal the floor with tile sealant to prevent the tiles (which are porous) from being stained with mortar. Use a paint roller to work the sealant over the surface of the tiles. After 30 minutes, mop up any excess with a clean sponge or cloth. Then leave to dry (ideally overnight).

Step 6

Lift an area of about 10 tiles in the corner furthest from the exit and begin to apply the mortar to the exposed section with the mason's trowel, spreading to a depth of about ½ in. (1.25cm).

Step 9

Remove any spacers. You can now begin to grout the tiles with the same mortar mix used for bonding. Mix up the mortar as described in Step 5, and work with a half-bucketful at a time. Start in a corner, and use a pointing trowel to pack the mortar into the joints, including around the edges. Try to avoid spilling too much onto the surface of the tiles.

Step 7

Lay the tiles from the walls inward, working toward the exit. Fit spacers between the tiles if required, and twist the tiles a little as you embed them in the mortar for better adhesion. Tap each tile down with a rubber mallet to expel any air beneath. Monitor the floor level as you go, using a carpenter's level (rest it on a straightedge if necessary). Lay more or less mortar as needed to compensate for thin or thick flags.

Step 10
Wipe excess mortar off the surface of the tiles with a damp sponge or cloth as you go. Wipe each tile once only, working diagonally across the tile, so you don't pull grout out of the joints. Rinse the sponge in clean water as needed, wringing well.

Step 11
When you've finished grouting and wiping the floor, go back to the beginning and smooth down the grout lines with a dowel or grouting tool. Leave the grout to set for 3 hours.

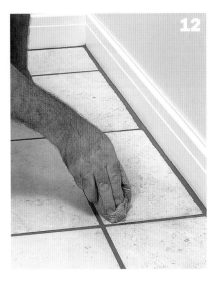

Step 12
Clean any smears of mortar from the surface of the tiles with a damp sponge or cloth. Let the mortar dry for at least 3 hours, then vacuum or sweep the floor. Apply another coat of tile sealant with a paint roller, working it well into the grout lines. Mop up any excess with a sponge and allow to dry, ideally overnight.

Step 13 (Areas where water is used)
A limestone or sandstone floor in a kitchen, bathroom or other room where water is used must be waterproofed by sealing the gaps between the tiles and the walls with caulking. Apply the caulking with a caulking gun, and leave to dry for at least 24 hours.

THE FLOORING LAYERS

Laying on a concrete subfloor

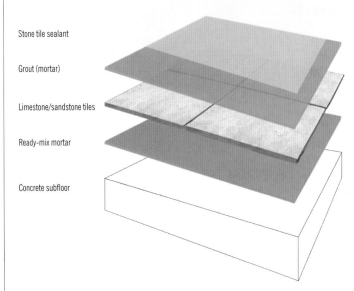

Stone tile sealant

Grout (mortar)

Limestone/sandstone tiles

Ready-mix mortar

Concrete subfloor

Laying on a wood subfloor

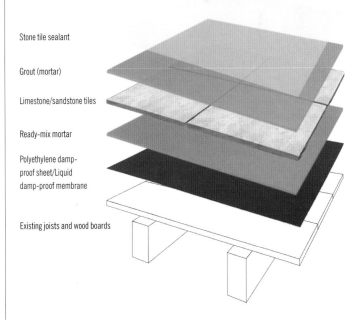

Stone tile sealant

Grout (mortar)

Limestone/sandstone tiles

Ready-mix mortar

Polyethylene damp-proof sheet/Liquid damp-proof membrane

Existing joists and wood boards

Brick

PROPERTIES AT A GLANCE
(*low, **medium, ***high)
- LOW MAINTENANCE ***
- HARD WEARING ***
- HEAT RETENTION **
- SOUND INSULATION *
- WATER RESISTANCE *

Brick has been used for building walls and floors for thousands of years. Molded from clay and fired, this is a less durable material than natural stone, but still hard-wearing and chosen also for its warmth (in appearance and to the touch) and its distinctively regular look. Brick is also less expensive than most hard tiles, and similarly easy to maintain.

You could conceivably use standard building bricks for flooring purposes, but these are very thick and not very durable. "Engineered bricks" have a longer life, but will still raise the height of the floor considerably. The best option is to use pavers, which are specially produced for flooring and range in width from around ¾–2 in. (2–5cm). Choose the thinner widths where possible to avoid excessive trimming of doors and fixtures, and discuss the options with your supplier.

Brick should really be installed over a concrete subfloor, especially when laid in a mortar bed (as this will add to the weight of the flooring). If you want to lay brick on a wood subfloor, ask a builder to confirm that the subfloor can take the load and use the thinnest pavers available. If you plan to use mortar over wood you must add a layer of waterproofing to prevent the water content of the mortar from rotting the wood. Seal pavers to make them waterproof; this process locks sand

Designing the floor

The pattern is the key to a brick floor's success—the distinctively regular shape of the pavers means that the eye immediately registers their layout. It is easy to create a variety of patterns. Running bond, with pavers laid in the same direction with staggered joints, is the easiest pattern to lay, and emphasizes the length or width of a room (depending on which way the pavers run). The diagonal lines of herringbone create an interesting decorative design, and this pattern is also straightforward to lay. Basketweave, with pavers laid in alternate horizontal and vertical groups, has a pleasing knotted effect. The pavers themselves sometimes incorporate simple decorative patterns in relief, such as diamonds or Maltese crosses.

Brick is usually earthy red, pink or brown, but sand-lime or calcium silicate bricks are also available, and these are pale in color (white, cream or soft pink) and so reflect more light than clay pavers. Pigments can be added to achieve colors such as blue or green. Different products produce different effects: the smooth orange pavers that might be associated with driveways create a contemporary look (especially with contrasting grouting), while a more weathered finish suits an old-fashioned setting.

Left: Often seen outside in the form of walls and terraces, bricks brought inside the home can lend a sense of the outdoors to living areas.

into the joints and gives the floor an attractive sheen. Some pavers, however, are already waterproof, and sealing is not necessary.

Maintenance

Sweep regularly or vacuum, and clean off dirt with a wet mop, using diluted household detergent. If you seal the floor, reapply the product as recommended—usually every 6 to 12 months. Don't overuse finishing products as these are not always required and may simply make the floor slippery.

Advantages
- Easy to maintain.
- Durable and waterproof.
- Warmer than most hard floors.
- Many options for creating striking patterns.
- Particularly suitable for kitchens, corridors, hallways and semi-outdoor areas such as verandahs.

Disadvantages
- Reduces room height.
- Not usually suitable for upper stories.

Right: Bricks reclaimed from old properties produce a visually interesting floor featuring uniquely weathered shapes and colors. This aged floor contrasts sharply with the pristine contemporary brickwork of the walls.

Below: Used for thousands of years, brick is perhaps the most traditional of flooring materials.

Laying a brick floor

A brick floor requires a firm, unyielding base, and is ideally installed on ground-level concrete. Bricks are either laid directly onto the subfloor, without adhesive or mortar, or into a wet mortar bed. The former method is the simplest, but mortar produces a stronger floor. If you want to install a brick floor on a wood subfloor, then the load factor must be considered carefully. It is possible to use ordinary bricks, but these are thicker and heavier than the flooring bricks called "pavers." Ordinary bricks will also erode quickly. Pavers come in a range of thicknesses, so use the thinner (and therefore lighter) versions. All types of brick will raise the level of the floor, so you will probably need to trim doors (☞ page 21).

Before you begin, remove existing floor coverings and prepare the subfloor. If you are fitting bricks into a mortar bed over a concrete or wood subfloor, you may omit the layer of leveling compound or marine plywood, as the mortar will smooth out irregularities. Bricks are best laid dry on a wood subfloor, but if you want wide joints you will need to use mortar (bear in mind that mortar will increase the weight of the floor considerably). In that case, you must protect the subfloor with a layer of polyethylene sheet or liquid damp-proof membrane—otherwise the water content of the mortar may rot the wood. If bricks are laid dry, with no mortar bed, you must level a concrete subfloor with leveling compound and cover wood boards with ¼ in. (6mm) marine plywood treated with diluted PVA adhesive (☞ pages 18–21 for instructions). Make a floor plan to calculate how many bricks you need, and map out your desired pattern (such as basketweave or herringbone) to ensure an even layout (☞ pages 12–15).

Golden rules
- Prepare the site before starting (☞ pages 18–21).
- Buy all materials at the same time to guarantee consistency and availability.
- Ask your supplier for advice, and follow the manufacturer's instructions.
- Work safely. Ventilate the room, and wear strong rubber gloves when working with mortar and sealer. Wear a mask, safety glasses, gloves and ear protectors when using power tools, and firmly secure bricks to be cut.

LEVEL OF DIFFICULTY
●●○○○
Bricks are small and light, and are easy to handle and split (although curves and notches are more tricky to cut). This method does not require bonding with either adhesive or mortar.

Toolbox
1 MASON'S LINE
2 TRY SQUARE
3 STRAIGHTEDGE
4 TILE SCORER, COLD CHISEL AND HAMMER
5 ANGLE GRINDER
6 MASONRY BIT AND HALF-ROUND FILE
7 DOWEL/GROUTING TOOL
8 WATERING CAN WITH FINE ROSE HEAD
9 VACUUM CLEANER/SOFT BROOM OR BRUSH
10 PAINT ROLLER
11 CLEAN CLOTHS (BURLAP)

Materials
12 BRICK PAVERS
13 CARD/KRAFT PAPER
14 MORTAR MIX (FOR GROUTING)
15 MASONRY SEALER

INSTALLING BRICKS WITHOUT MORTAR

Preparing the bricks

Sort the bricks for tonal variations, and stack them in piles placed conveniently around the room. Unlike other hard floors, bricks are not laid out according to the quarter method because they are rectangular and often laid in a staggered pattern. Also, since bricks are relatively small, irregularities at the walls are less noticeable. Start laying from the longest, straightest wall, and follow your plan. If your walls are not straight and parallel to the room, attach a mason's line to two loose bricks and stretch it out at a brick's width from the wall. This will give you both a straight edge and a height level. If the wall is very angled, use a try square to establish a straight line at a brick's width from one corner. Mark the line on the floor using a straightedge, and extend it to the other side of the room with a mason's line.

Step 1
Lay the first course of bricks along the mason's line (or the wall if it is straight enough), butting them together tightly. Continue using the mason's line, realigning if necessary, for at least three courses until you have a firm block to push new rows against.

Step 2
Cut and fit edge bricks (☞ pages 26–27), allowing for a ⅛ in. (3mm) grouting gap at the wall. Use card or Kraft paper templates to shape bricks around pipes, vents and corners (☞ page 27). Split bricks with a tile scorer, cold chisel and hammer, and cut curves with an angle grinder. You can drill holes using a masonry bit, smoothing with a half-round file.

Step 3
Once the floor is completely covered, you need to grout the bricks. Sprinkle dry mortar mix (available premixed from building suppliers) over the surface, and use a soft broom to sweep the mix into the joints, including around the room's edges, brushing in different directions as you go. Repeat this twice daily for the next few days so that all the spaces between the bricks are filled.

Step 4
Use a dowel or grouting tool to score along the joints, pressing the mix firmly into the gaps.

Step 5
To create a bond, water the floor, using a watering can with a fine rose head, until you can see the water being absorbed into the mortar mix. Leave to dry for 24 hours.

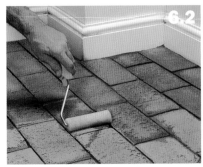

Step 6
Sweep or vacuum up any surplus mortar mix. Apply masonry sealer to the floor with a paint roller, working it into the surface of the bricks and the joints. Mop up any excess sealer with a clean cloth 30 minutes after application, and leave to dry overnight.

THE FLOORING LAYERS

Laying without mortar on a concrete subfloor

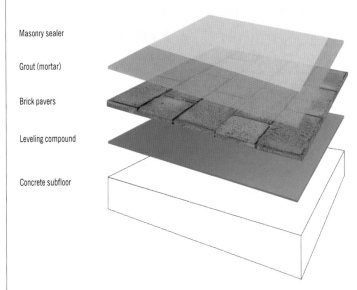

Masonry sealer

Grout (mortar)

Brick pavers

Leveling compound

Concrete subfloor

Laying without mortar on a wood subfloor

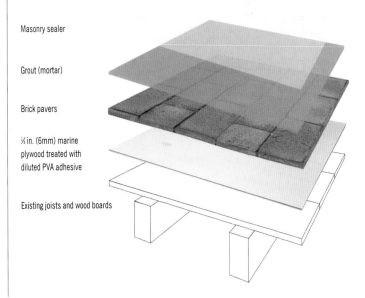

Masonry sealer

Grout (mortar)

Brick pavers

¼ in. (6mm) marine plywood treated with diluted PVA adhesive

Existing joists and wood boards

INSTALLING BRICKS WITH MORTAR

LEVEL OF DIFFICULTY

●●●○○

This method is harder than laying bricks directly onto the subfloor, as you are working with mortar, which sets quickly. You also need to use a mason's line throughout the installation to keep the grouting gaps consistent and the floor level.

Toolbox

1 MASON'S LINE
2 TILE SCORER, COLD CHISEL AND HAMMER
3 ANGLE GRINDER
4 MASONRY BIT AND HALF-ROUND FILE
5 BRICK TROWEL
6 WHISK (OPTIONAL)
7 RUBBER MALLET
8 CARPENTER'S LEVEL
9 STRAIGHTEDGE
10 CLEAN CLOTHS (BURLAP)
11 POINTING TROWEL
12 DOWEL/GROUTING TOOL
13 VACUUM CLEANER/SOFT BRUSH OR BROOM
14 PAINT ROLLER

Materials

15 BRICK PAVERS
16 POLYETHYLENE DAMP-PROOF SHEET/LIQUID DAMP-PROOF MEMBRANE (FOR A WOOD SUBFLOOR)
17 CARD/KRAFT PAPER
18 MORTAR MIX
19 ⅛ IN. (3MM) POLYETHYLENE SHEET
20 MASONRY SEALER

Preparing the bricks

As for *Installing bricks without mortar* (☞ page 60). It is essential to install waterproofing over a wood subfloor (☞ page 19). You will need to use a mason's line throughout this method, even if your walls are straight, in order to keep the grouting spaces consistent and the floor level.

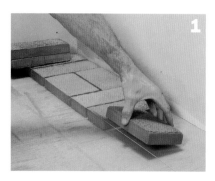

Step 1
Lay the first course dry along the mason's line, leaving gaps of ¼–½ in. (6mm–1.25cm) for grouting (depending on the desired effect). Realign the mason's line for each course to ensure consistent spacing. Follow your floor plan: if you are laying a basketweave pattern, your first course will comprise bricks laid in different directions, as shown here.

Step 2
Cut and fit the edge bricks as described in Step 2 of *Installing bricks without mortar* (☞ page 60).

Step 3
Once the floor is covered, mix up a quantity of mortar. Add water to the mortar mix (available premixed from building suppliers), mixing with a brick trowel or whisk until you achieve a creamy consistency. Mix up no more than you can use in an hour—start with half a bucketful.

Step 4
Lift about 15 bricks in the corner furthest from the exit and apply the mortar to the exposed section with the trowel, spreading to a depth of around ½ in. (1.25cm) and combing slightly.

Step 5
Lay the bricks from the walls inward, working toward the exit. Twist each brick a little as you embed it in the mortar for better adhesion. Tap each brick down with a rubber mallet to expel any air beneath. Monitor the floor level as you go, using a carpenter's level (rest it on a straightedge if necessary).

Step 6
Lift another section of about 15 bricks and continue in the same way until you have worked your way across the floor to the exit. Try not to kneel or walk on newly laid bricks, and wipe off surplus mortar with a piece of damp burlap as you go. Leave to set for at least 3 hours.

Step 7

Once the mortar is dry, you can begin to grout the bricks, with the same mortar mix used for fixing. Mix up the mortar as described in Step 3, and work with a half-bucketful at a time. Start in a corner, and use a pointing trowel to pack the mortar into the joints, including around the room's edges. Try to avoid spilling too much mortar onto the surface of the bricks.

Step 8

Wipe excess mortar off the surface of the bricks with a piece of damp burlap as you go. Wipe each brick only once, working the cloth diagonally across the brick, to avoid pulling grout out of the joints. Rinse the burlap in clean water as needed.

Step 9

When you've finished grouting and wiping the whole floor, go back to the beginning and smooth down the grout lines with a dowel or grouting tool. Leave the grout to set for at least 3 hours.

Step 10

Clean up any excess mortar with a piece of damp burlap. Cover the whole floor with a ⅛ in. (3mm) polyethylene sheet, and leave for 4 days. (Avoid walking on the floor for at least 24 hours, and tread gently afterward.) Then remove the sheet and allow the floor to dry completely before sealing—this can take over a month. Premature sealing will trap moisture in the brick and discolor the surface.

Step 11

Vacuum or sweep the floor to remove any particles of dust or grit. Then seal the floor with masonry sealer, working it over the surface of the bricks and into the grout lines using a paint roller. After 30 minutes, wipe up any excess sealer with a clean cloth, and leave to dry overnight. Replace moldings and baseboards as necessary.

THE FLOORING LAYERS

Laying with mortar on a concrete subfloor

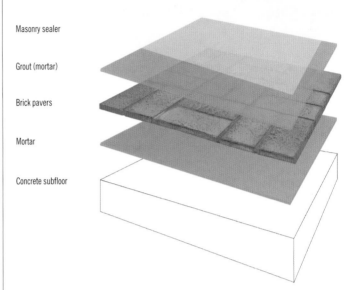

Masonry sealer

Grout (mortar)

Brick pavers

Mortar

Concrete subfloor

Laying with mortar on a wood subfloor

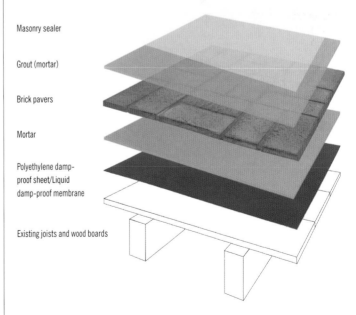

Masonry sealer

Grout (mortar)

Brick pavers

Mortar

Polyethylene damp-proof sheet/Liquid damp-proof membrane

Existing joists and wood boards

CALLING IN THE PROFESSIONALS
Marble and granite

PROPERTIES AT A GLANCE
(*low, **medium, ***high)
HARD-WEARING ***
WATER RESISTANCE ***
LOW MAINTENANCE **
HEAT RETENTION *
SOUND INSULATION *

Smooth and hard, cool to the touch and beautifully patterned, there's a certain magic about marble and granite that just can't be reproduced by other materials, and certainly not by any synthetic simulation. These are not cheap floors to install as the materials are expensive and you will need to employ a professional fitter to achieve the perfectly smooth, level and tightly aligned finish that is required, but the result will be a classically spectacular floor that will last a lifetime. Attempting to lay marble or granite yourself would be a false economy: the high price of the materials raises the cost of mistakes, and installation requires the use of specialist tools.

Marble is most commonly found in bathrooms, where the smaller size of the room makes such a luxurious floor more affordable. Bear in mind that a marble floor in a bathroom must be sealed. Granite is waterproof and provides an excellent alternative for bathrooms. It is important, however, to obtain professional advice as to whether the subfloor can take the weight of the planned floor—granite in particular will be too heavy for an ordinary suspended wood subfloor. If not, you will need to employ a builder to reinforce the floor (which is expensive) or choose a lighter covering. Marble and granite also make a fabulous formal floor for a hallway or reception room.

Unless you live in a year-round hot climate, where these floorings offer a welcome cooling effect, consider installing underfloor heating.

Maintenance
Granite is extremely tough and does not require special care beyond regular sweeping and wiping, but handle marble gently. You should sweep the floor with a soft broom and clean off dirt with a damp mop, using diluted household detergent. Work in sections so that the detergent solution is never on the floor for long. Don't use harsh abrasive cleaners on marble as these will take away the shine and may cause discoloration. Marble must be treated with sealant during installation or it will stain; reapply coats according to the manufacturer's instructions. Granite is waterproof but can be sealed if you require a more polished appearance.

What to watch out for
- Choose a reputable installation company and ask for customer recommendations.
- If you would like a certain design, make sure that the installer is willing to work with your ideas.

Designing the floor

Marble and granite are available in a wide range of colors and exhibit distinctive imperfections that often contrast strongly with the background color. Marble is randomly patterned with delicate or bold veins, streaks and "clouds," and granite is more uniformly speckled or blotched. You can also buy plain marble or granite, but the appeal of these materials often lies in their imperfections. Marble is available in shades of white, cream, pink, red, green, blue, gray and black, and granite is supplied in similar colors. The best marble is traditionally from Italy, but it is also quarried elsewhere, and the source will determine the coloring.

You can commission a layout to make the most of the contrasting colors and patterns available, perhaps installing a 3-D or classical checkerboard design. Slabs can be cut in a range of shapes to fit together perfectly. For a very modern setting, granite and marble may be supplied with minimal patterning in a sleek, burnished style. The flooring can have a gloss finish or a more aged effect (with marble this is called "tumbled"), which may be more suitable for smaller spaces and provide some slip resistance for bathrooms.

GRAY MARBLE

BEIGE MARBLE

GREEN MARBLE

YELLOW MARBLE

Left: Hard-wearing and timeless, marble is perfect for use in hallways and foyers. This classic checkerboard design has been made even more striking by the addition of a large motif.

Right: This kitchen floor has been given a rustic, aged look with tumbled marble tiles.

- Ask for confirmation that the subfloor can take the weight of the floor.
- Check with the supplier that the stone will come from the same batch.
- Examine individual slabs to judge how color, grain and veining will match.
- Make sure marble is sealed to protect it from staining.

Advantages
- Beautiful random patterning and marvelous smoothness.
- Extremely durable.
- Water-resistant (if marble is sealed).
- Creates a very luxurious effect.
- Particularly suitable for bathrooms, hallways, conservatories and formal living areas.

Disadvantages
- Expensive.
- Marble can stain and is not water-resistant unless sealed.
- Cold and hard.

THE FLOORING LAYERS

Laying on a concrete subfloor

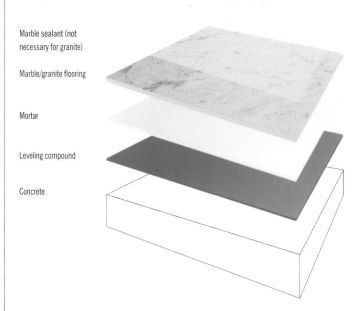

Marble sealant (not necessary for granite)

Marble/granite flooring

Mortar

Leveling compound

Concrete

Laying on a wood subfloor

Marble sealant

Marble flooring (granite is too heavy for a wood subfloor)

Hard floor-tile adhesive

¼ in. (6mm) marine plywood treated with diluted PVA adhesive

Existing joists and wood boards

Below: The variety of color in these small blue marble tiles gives the floor an interesting mosaic-like appearance.

CALLING IN THE PROFESSIONALS
Terrazzo

PROPERTIES AT A GLANCE
(*low, **medium, ***high)
HARD WEARING ***
WATER RESISTANCE ***
LOW MAINTENANCE ***
HEAT RETENTION *
SOUND INSULATION *

The cost of the material and the need for professional installation make terrazzo one of the most expensive types of hard flooring, but it is increasingly the floor of choice in ultra-modern settings such as warehouse conversions, thanks to a chic industrial aesthetic combined with durability and ease of maintenance.

Sometimes known as Venetian mosaic, terrazzo consists of stone chippings (often marble or granite) laid in concrete or resin. The material is spread on site and, when the concrete or resin has set, the surface of the floor is machine-ground and polished for the perfectly smooth finish that is characteristic of terrazzo. This process brings out the color of the stone chippings and produces a bright and seamless floor, but is very difficult and best left to the professionals. Terrazzo tiles are also available, but they too need grinding and polishing, and are not recommended for installation by nonprofessionals. To avoid movement of the subfloor leading to unsightly cracking, the fitter will need to ensure that the subfloor is perfectly rigid and smooth, and install expansion strips to minimize the risk of cracking. If you are planning to install terrazzo on a wood subfloor, ask a contractor to confirm that the floor can take the weight of the mortar.

The smooth shininess of terrazzo works well in an airy open setting such as a conservatory or large hallway. It is easily cleaned, waterproof and durable, so is also ideal for bathrooms, and can be used for a contemporary look in living areas. Terrazzo is popular in Mediterranean regions as a means of keeping houses cool in summer, but consider underfloor heating if you live in a chillier climate.

Maintenance
The smoothness of terrazzo makes it very easy to wipe clean. Sweep the floor regularly with a soft broom, and mop with diluted household detergent. Add shine using a product recommended by your supplier to avoid making the floor dangerously slippery with an unsuitable finish.

What to watch out for
• Choose a reputable installation company and ask for customer recommendations.

Designing the floor
A terrazzo floor usually creates a smooth, highly polished look that works best in very contemporary interiors, but it can also be used to produce a grand, luxurious feel, in a vestibule or large bathroom, for example. The placement, coloring and size of the chips vary, resulting in a good choice of different patterns and textures. A softer shape of chip results in a floor that resembles marble; sharper, smaller chips can produce the appearance of mosaic.

To create a truly original floor, ask your suppliers to install motifs produced to your design specifications. Popular motifs include images of stars, fish or ships, and various geometric designs. If the terrazzo is spread on site (rather than supplied as tiles), there are further possibilities for manipulating the color and distribution of the chips, and even adding other materials into the mix. Terrazzo can also work very well (and more cheaply) as an inset strip that contrasts with other flooring materials.

AQUAMARINE

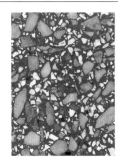

AGATE

JET

AMETHYST

Resin floors
Similar to terrazzo but without the inclusion of stone chippings, this hard-wearing industrial-looking surface is suitable for kitchens, conservatories and areas of heavy use. The floor is poured on site, either as large areas of flat color or in simple abstract patterns.

• As terrazzo is laid in mortar, any plywood underlayment must be waterproofed with polyethylene sheet or liquid damp-proof membrane to prevent the water content of the mortar from rotting the wood.

• Ask for confirmation that the subfloor can take the weight of the floor.

Advantages
• Extremely durable and easy to maintain.
• Water-resistant.
• A sophisticated, contemporary look.
• Particularly suitable for hallways, kitchens, conservatories, living rooms and bathrooms.

Disadvantages
• Expensive.
• Difficult to remove if your tastes change.
• Cold, hard and noisy.

Right: Contemporary designers are increasingly borrowing flooring materials from commercial or industrial settings and reinterpreting them in a domestic context.

THE FLOORING LAYERS

Laying on a concrete subfloor

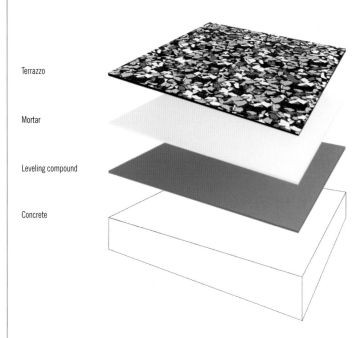

Terrazzo

Mortar

Leveling compound

Concrete

Laying on a wood subfloor

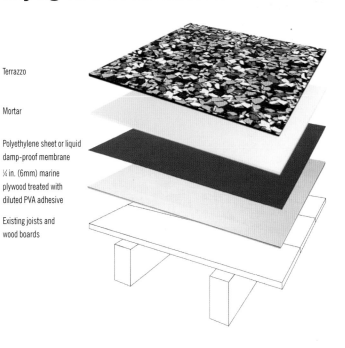

Terrazzo

Mortar

Polyethylene sheet or liquid damp-proof membrane

¼ in. (6mm) marine plywood treated with diluted PVA adhesive

Existing joists and wood boards

CALLING IN THE PROFESSIONALS
Metal

PROPERTIES AT A GLANCE

(*low, **medium, ***high)

HARD WEARING ***

WATER RESISTANCE ***

LOW MAINTENANCE **

HEAT RETENTION *

SOUND INSULATION *

You can't get smarter than a shiny silver floor in stainless steel or aluminum sheeting. The material is not cheap and you will need to employ professional labor as the cutting, drilling and welding techniques involved are beyond the scope of the amateur—but for those seeking a sophisticated industrial look the stunningly contemporary results will justify the cost. Metal floors are supplied as tiles, sheets or planks. They are usually made from aluminum or steel, but can be given the look of brass, copper, bronze and other metals. These floors are often made from recycled materials (check with your supplier about the specific product you are buying).

Metal can be laid on both concrete and wood subfloors without trouble (if you are worried about the strength of the subfloor, choose aluminum, which is lighter than steel). The flooring is usually screwed and plugged, but can also be glued. If using screws, the installer should also apply a little adhesive to dampen rattle, although this won't stop a metal floor from being noisy. A harsh utilitarian effect, however, can be part of the charm of this type of flooring. Many metal floors are textured to provide slip resistance, which is especially useful if you are flooring an area where water will be present, such as a kitchen or bathroom.

Maintenance

Sweep metal floors regularly to remove abrasive particles, and wash them with a mop, using diluted household detergent. A highly polished look can be desirable but repeated polishing may make the floor dangerously slippery. Talk to your supplier about nonslip burnishing products.

What to watch out for

- Choose a reputable installation company and ask for customer recommendations.
- Ask for confirmation that the subfloor can take the weight of the floor.
- Check whether the flooring is made from recycled materials.

COPPER

GOLD

SILVER

VERDIGRIS

Designing the floor

Metal is usually chosen to fit with a contemporary theme, but you are not confined to a moody industrial look. You could certainly install a grated or studded factory-style floor, but you can also choose from a range of metallic hues, including bronze, copper, gold and silver, to add a fairy-tale sparkle to the room. Companies produce a range of contrasting metal inset tiles, featuring motifs such as flowers, stars, swirls, animal prints and fish, and will even create motifs to your own design. A metal floor will lend an airy sense of space to a room, and can be used to lighten dark areas. This lightening effect will be increased if you incorporate glass tiles into the floor, and you could also choose to mix metal with other materials, such as marble or wood. To fine-tune the décor, take your pick from a variety of finishes: metal coverings are supplied in satin, mirror, laquered or matte finishes (or in a combination of these).

IRON

Opposite: A silver-effect aluminum floor with embossed inset tiles is wonderfully decorative and, being waterproof and durable, practical too.

Right: Textured studs not only add interest to the metal but also allow the flooring to be polished to a high gloss without losing its nonslip properties.

- If you would like a certain design, make sure that the installer is willing to work with your ideas.
- Decide whether you need nonslip texturing.

Advantages
- Durable.
- Water-resistant.
- Ultra-contemporary look that brightens dark areas.
- Particularly suitable for modern living spaces, kitchens, hallways and walkways.

Disadvantages
- Expensive.
- Hard, noisy and cold.

THE FLOORING LAYERS

Laying on a concrete subfloor

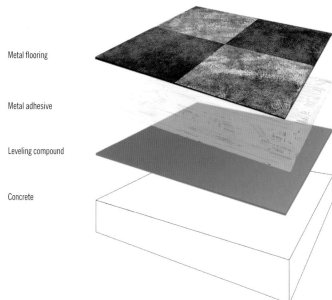

Metal flooring

Metal adhesive

Leveling compound

Concrete

Laying on a wood subfloor

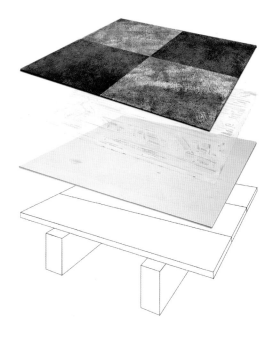

Metal flooring

Metal adhesive

¼ in. (6mm) marine plywood treated with diluted PVA adhesive

Existing joists and wood boards

CALLING IN THE PROFESSIONALS
Glass

PROPERTIES AT A GLANCE
(*low, **medium, ***high)
WATER RESISTANCE ***
HARD WEARING **
LOW MAINTENANCE *
HEAT RETENTION *
SOUND INSULATION *

A sheer glass floor allows natural light to flood through the building, and simultaneously makes a significant design statement. Perhaps the most spectacular of all floors, glass is correspondingly expensive and difficult to install. This is not a floor that can be installed by an amateur. The subfloor, including the joists, is entirely removed, and the glass panels are suspended in a metal framework. A project engineer will be required to calculate precisely the loading of the glass. Glass floors are custom-built to the requirements of the site, so you will need to find a specialist installer. It is advisable to choose a product with a slip-resistant coating or texturing on the surface.

Glass tiles can be used in mosaic, as a feature in tiled floors such as ceramic and even to add interest to a concrete floor, but check that the tiles are suitable for use as flooring (some are too brittle and slippery). They are supplied in a range of sizes, from tesserae to brick-shaped pavers, and are installed as you would lay the main material of the floor. Bear in mind that an entire floor covered with these tiles would probably be too slippery unless textured. Many glass tiles are now recycled from used drinks bottles, and these display interesting flaws in the form of bubbles and cracks.

Maintenance

Avoid scratching your glass floor. Sweep it regularly with a soft broom to remove abrasive particles, and clean off dirt with a mop and diluted household detergent. You will need to clean

Designing the floor

Sheer glass will make the floor feel as if it is floating in mid-air, and add extra sophistication to a minimalist interior. A glass staircase can be particularly striking, seemingly ascending without any means of support. There are also many different ways in which you can combine glass panels with other flooring materials, such as metal or marble, perhaps using the glass to distribute light to a landing or display art or other objects. A range of tints and colors are available, and you could even have the surface of the glass etched with a design of your choice. Find a specialist company who will be able to talk through the many design options open to you.

the floor frequently in order to maintain its pristine condition. Ask your supplier for a recommended nonslip sealant to avoid making the floor dangerously slippery with polish.

What to watch out for

- Choose a reputable installation company and ask for customer recommendations.
- Ask whether the glass is recycled.
- Make sure the installers are willing to explore the many design options available.
- Talk to the supplier about antislip texturing and nonslip products for maintenance.

Advantages

- Creates a wonderfully artistic effect.
- Adds light to the setting.
- Durable and water-resistant.
- Particularly suitable for upstairs living rooms, stairways, halls and bathrooms.

Disadvantages

- Very expensive.
- Cold and hard.
- Can be slippery.

Left: Opaque glass tiles bring both translucence and privacy to a very contemporary bedroom.

Above: Mirrors, glass flooring and underfloor lighting create an environment where nothing is quite as it first appears to be.

Right: Glass flooring can be used to great effect in small areas, giving the illusion of space and depth and increasing the available light in the room.

THE FLOORING LAYERS

Glass panels

Suspended metal framework

RESILIENT FLOORS

Originally widely popular for ease of maintenance, comfort and value for money, resilient floorings such as linoleum and vinyl now also offer colors, designs and effects to suit every budget and setting. You can buy vinyl that mimics slate or wood, make use of border strips or inset tiles, or even order a custom-made linoleum floor featuring an original motif of your choice. Rubber is an excitingly contemporary floor, supplied in an ever-increasing spectrum of colors, while cork creates a warm and natural atmosphere that suits any home. Leather is the ultimate in luxury—and correspondingly expensive. Resilient tiles are among the easiest floors to install, but be warned that linoleum and vinyl sheet are very hard for the amateur to lay successfully.

Installing resilient floors

Resilient floors, which are available as tiles and as sheet vinyl or linoleum, are thinner and softer than other floors, meaning that the smallest imperfection in the subfloor will show through. Tiled resilient floors are among the easiest floors to lay, but sheet vinyl and linoleum are much harder to install since sheet is difficult to maneuver and fit around the edges with a professional effect. Removing moldings, baseboards and vent grills is recommended when laying sheet to ensure neater edges. Bear in mind that linoleum sheet seams are sealed with a heat gun, which is not recommended for use by amateurs.

How suitable is the subfloor?

Resilient floors are light enough to be laid without problem on suspended wood subfloors. It is, however, essential that the subfloor be smooth and level. Wood floorboards should be leveled with ¼ in. (6mm) marine plywood, and concrete subfloors with leveling compound (☞ pages 18–19). If you are laying leather, it is recommended that a wood or concrete subfloor be covered with ¾ in. (2cm) plywood to ensure a solid base for these expensive tiles. Talk to your supplier about the recommended underlayment for your floor.

Acclimatizing flooring

All resilient flooring benefits from being stored on site and at room temperature before installation. This enables vinyl, cork, rubber, leather and particularly linoleum, which are brittle when cold, to warm up and become more flexible and less prone to cracking. It is also vital to allow linoleum and cork, which are wood-based products and will expand or contract in response to sudden changes in ambient temperature or humidity, time to stabilize in the new conditions. Keep the room warm and store vinyl, leather and rubber on site for at least 24 hours before installation. Linoleum and cork should be kept on site for at least 48 hours before installation.

Tiles or sheet?

Tiles are much easier to handle than sheet of any kind, and don't require jointing, which is a time-consuming and tricky technique that compromises the water resistance of sheet flooring. It is also difficult to cut the edges of a sheet to fit the room perfectly; you will need to make a template that includes all the room's edges to ensure a successful installation. You might even want to make a template of the entire floor before cutting the sheet. If, however, you are able to remove all the furniture and fixtures from the room, and don't have to deal with awkward recesses and pipes, sheet flooring can be quicker and tidier to install than tiles.

PREPARING THE ROOM

Since resilient tiles are relatively easy to cut and shape to fit around the edges of a room, it is not recommended that you risk damaging moldings, baseboards or fixtures by removing them before installation. Sheet flooring, however, is more difficult to cut to fit precisely, and it is a good idea to remove moldings, baseboards and floor vent grills, and replace them after the floor is laid. Some installers will go so far as to completely remove floor-mounted fixtures such as the toilet, but this can be a disruptive procedure. A toilet, for example, is often attached to the floor with a wax seal that must be reinstalled when the toilet is replaced. A better option in this case would be to cut the flooring to fit and then seal the edges with caulking.

Step 1
Moldings or baseboards can be removed with a pry bar and cold chisel (taking care not to damage them) and re-installed with glue or nails after the floor is laid.

Step 2
If your toilet is not attached to the floor with a wax seal, you can turn off the water supply and loosen the bolts of the toilet bowl to slide the sheet as far under it as you can.

Step 3
Some bath panels may be unscrewed so that sheet flooring can be installed under the bath. This helps prevent water from seeping under the sheeting and causing the floor to lift or curl. If your bathtub unit is tiled in, your best option is to seal the edge between floor and fixture with caulking. You can also attach a decorative base molding to the fixture to hide the edges of the sheet.

TECHNIQUES FOR RESILIENT FLOORS

It is essential that you use the recommended adhesive for your floor—failure to do so will result in the manufacturer's warranty becoming invalid. Always ask your supplier for advice when buying adhesive, caulking or any products used for maintenance.

Before you start, make a plan of your floor layout, including any linear or geometric patterns (☛ pages 12–15). If you want to install a border of contrasting tiles, lay out the tiles following the border method

(☛ page 15). If you are laying tiles with a marbled or grain effect, rotate each tile through 90 degrees from the position of the last tile. This creates a more natural effect. Always lay the whole floor out dry before fixing tiles to judge the overall effect.

Take care when laying the floor not to trap adhesive between tiles. Excess adhesive may create unsightly bulges at the seams. Instead, to adjust placement, lift and re-place tiles individually.

Cutting resilient flooring

Unlike hard tiles, which often require powerful cutting tools, resilient flooring can be cut with just a utility knife. Buy a good one, with extra blades. Curved linoleum blades are useful for tougher materials such as linoleum or rubber, but can be difficult to use with a straightedge. Score with a utility knife and straightedge first, then cut using the linoleum blade.

USEFUL TIP
Heating up a resilient tile with a hair dryer before attempting a complex cut will make the tile more pliable and easier to cut.

Step 1
When you reach the edge of the room, lay a loose tile on top of the last whole tile.

Step 2
Place another tile on top of this and push it over the space between the whole tile and the wall.

Step 3
Mark a cutting line on the middle tile by drawing along the edge of the top tile. Use a try square to draw true lines from your measurements. Cut along the line using a utility knife and straightedge. This will be your edge tile.

The step-by-step instructions to installing rubber tiles (☛ pages 92–93) demonstrate how to use templates to shape resilient tiles at corners and around obstacles such as bathroom fixtures. If you are laying vinyl with grout feature strip, remember to allow for the "grout" gap between tiles and around the walls when you are calculating the width of the edge tiles.

USEFUL TIP
Try to avoid cutting tiles on top of already laid tiles as you may damage their surface. Cut tiles on a scrap piece of plywood instead.

Joining sheets

Cut linoleum or vinyl sheet in a room larger than the area of your site. You should leave sheets taped together, overlapping by about 1 in. (2.5cm), until all the edge cuts have been made using a template of the site's perimeter. Then create a perfect joint by cutting through both sheets at the same time, using a straightedge. Use a pattern line as a cutting guide or measure from the edge of the flooring and join up the marks with a straightedge. Then transport the cut sheets to the site for gluing. Linoleum seams are sealed once the adhesive has set (at least 10 hours after installation). Groove joints with a router and use a heat gun (which can be rented) to melt welding rod (thin strips of linoleum) into the seams.

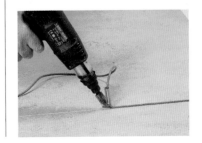

Vinyl

PROPERTIES AT A GLANCE

(*low, **medium, ***high)

- **LOW MAINTENANCE** ***
- **HARD-WEARING** **
- **HEAT RETENTION** **
- **SOUND INSULATION** **
- **WATER RESISTANCE** **

Vinyl—also referred to as PVC vinyl—is manufactured in sheet and tile form. It is not the same product as true linoleum (☞ pages 86–87). Vinyl is available in a variety of grades and prices, from cheap and relatively shortlived material to more expensive flooring with greater durability. Easy to clean and water resistant, vinyl is a practical choice, and the huge range of colors and designs on the market should ensure that you find a flooring that suits your style and budget.

Vinyl tiles tend to provide greater creative flexibility than vinyl sheet, offering potential for using feature strips and borders, and mixing different colors and motifs. Tiles can also be more economical when standard sheet sizes do not match the floor area, which may result in substantial waste. Sheet vinyl offers more protection against spills than tiles, except around the edges (wood-effect vinyl is particularly suitable for wet areas where natural wood or laminate might not be

appropriate). Vinyl sheet incorporates a PVC cushion layer, which can make it more comfortable underfoot than vinyl tiling. However, dropping a sharp object such as a knife on sheet vinyl can result in a visible puncture exposing the white cushioning below the surface.

Tiles are much easier to lay than sheet, which is difficult to fit at the edges. If you have some experience, however, and are flooring a simply shaped room, sheet can be quicker and less messy to lay. Sheet is cut to length as required and supplied in a wider range of widths than linoleum, meaning that you may be able to avoid joining pieces. Tiles are square, and can be bought in a variety of sizes, to suit the size and layout of the room. Some "wood-look" products are supplied as planks, which you lay as you would install vinyl tiles.

You can buy self-stick tiles, which are installed without a layer of adhesive, but these tend to be poor quality and are not

SLATE-EFFECT TILES

SHEET WITH GROUTED TERRA-COTTA EFFECT

Designing the floor

Vinyl flooring is available in a range of colors, plain or patterned, and in a variety of natural effects including wood-look products, which mimic just about every kind of wood, and a selection of simulated hard floors, from mosaic to terra-cotta, sandstone and marble. Whether these simulated products are successful or not is a matter of opinion. A laminate floor is probably a more realistic imitation of a natural wood floor, and remember that a vinyl stone-look floor is neither cold nor hard, which may be of benefit to some people but lessens the effect. What is undeniable, however, is that the more you spend on vinyl, the better the effect. It's well worth obtaining a sample piece rather than relying on a brochure to judge the quality of the simulation.

A vinyl floor offers great opportunity for creativity. You can buy tiles with decorative borders or motifs, and contrasting colors or patterns laid out boldly across the floor will look striking. Certain tiles give a diagonal-lay effect. Many different border strips are available, as well as feature strips to fit between tiles to highlight an area of tiling or create a simulation of a grouted floor. And if you don't want to go to the bother of laying individual tiles and grout strips, then simply buy vinyl sheet with a built-in grouted-tile effect.

Left: Vinyl comes in a wide range of hard-floor effects, which are supplied as individual tiles and also as sheets that simulate grouted tiles.

Right: Vinyl planks, tiles and sheets are often provided with design features such as borders and diagonal-lay effects.

OAK-EFFECT PLANK

TILE WITH BORDER AND DIAGONAL-LAY EFFECT

MOSAIC-EFFECT TILE WITH BORDER

recommended. Also available is "perimeter-bond" sheet, glued around edges and seams only. This product is also not recommended as it does not produce as secure a floor as the "fully-bonded" sheet described in this book.

Maintenance

Vinyl floors are easy to clean—some even come with a built-in soil inhibitor! Sweep vinyl gently with a soft broom to remove abrasive particles of dirt that can damage the surface. Wash the floor with a sponge mop, using diluted household detergent. Keep the mop damp rather than sopping wet, and make sure it is clean to avoid scratching the floor. Your supplier will offer special products for cleaning and enhancing vinyl flooring. Vinyl floor enhancer really does make the surface of vinyl glow. It can be applied every few months, but you will need to cut back the build-up of dirt and enhancer every year or so using a stripping product.

Advantages
- Practical and easy to maintain.
- Supplied in a price range to suit all budgets.
- Excellent availability and a wide range of design options.
- Copes well with moisture.
- Particularly suited for kitchens, bathrooms and laundry and utility rooms.

Disadvantages
- Can wear quickly in high-traffic areas.
- Lighter colors show dirt readily.
- Does not always simulate natural materials effectively.
- Manufactured from synthetic materials and not as environmentally friendly as natural floors, including true linoleum.

Above: "Wood-look" vinyl planks create a warm atmosphere, and are easier to clean and maintain than real wood.

Above: The more expensive vinyl products offer an impressive range of simulations. Here, vinyl provides a striking imitation of a decorative stone floor.

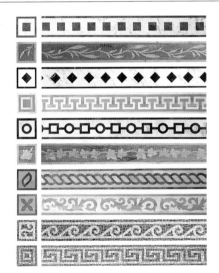

DECORATIVE BORDERS

CARTWHEEL FEATURE

Laying a vinyl floor

LEVEL OF DIFFICULTY

●○○○○

Vinyl tiles are light, and easy to cut and lay. Laying feature strips of fake grout between the tiles, however, can be a fiddly job.

Toolbox

1 CHALK LINE
2 PAINTER'S TAPE
3 UTILITY KNIFE
4 RULER
5 ⅛ IN. (3MM)
    NOTCHED TROWEL
6 LINOLEUM ROLLER
7 CLEAN CLOTHS/SPONGES
8 CAULKING GUN (FOR WET
    AREAS ONLY)

Materials

9 VINYL TILES
10 GROUT FEATURE
    STRIPS (OPTIONAL)
11 KRAFT PAPER/CARD
12 VINYL FLOOR
    TILE ADHESIVE
13 CAULKING (FOR WET
    AREAS ONLY)

Before you begin laying your vinyl floor, remove existing floor coverings. It is not advisable to leave any resilient floors in place (as they can come loose, causing the floor above to lift), but avoid in particular laying vinyl on vinyl, as a chemical reaction between the two can cause a yellow stain on the surface of the top layer. Vinyl is thinner than other resilient flooring (although vinyl sheet has an extra layer of cushioning that makes it thicker than vinyl tiles), so it is essential to ensure that the subfloor is clean and smooth. Level a concrete subfloor with leveling compound and cover wood floorboards with ¼ in. (6mm) marine plywood treated with diluted PVA adhesive. If you want extra insulation, consider installing insulating panels, which are used in place of plywood (☛ pages 18–21 for instructions for preparing the site).

Make a floor plan to calculate how many tiles you need, and map out any design to ensure an accurate layout (☛ pages 12–15). When installing vinyl sheet, bear in mind that it is worth buying a wider sheet than needed, and wasting some, in order to cover the area without making a seam.

Golden rules

- Prepare the site before starting (☛ pages 18–21), taking special care to ensure a level subfloor.
- Buy all materials at the same time.
- Ask your supplier for advice, and follow the manufacturer's instructions.
- Work safely. Ventilate the room well and wear strong rubber gloves when working with adhesive and caulking.

INSTALLING VINYL TILES

Preparing the tiles

Increase the pliability of the vinyl by keeping the room warm and the tiles on site for at least 24 hours before installation. Sort the tiles for variations in color and pattern, and stack them in piles placed conveniently around the room. Mark two chalk lines at right angles through the center of the room, to act as guides in laying out the floor, and adjust them according to the quarter method (☛ page 14). If you would like a border of contrasting tiles, start by laying this out first (☛ page 15).

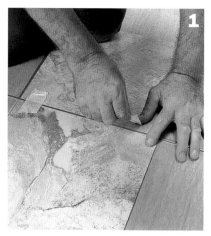

Step 1

If you are using feature strips of ⅛ in. (3mm) wide fake grout, lay these first along the adjusted chalk lines. Then lay the tiles dry along the cross, fitting them closely together and holding them in place with short strips of painter's tape. Now fill in the four quarters, working from the center of the room toward the walls, until the entire floor except the edges is laid out in a dry run. As you work, twist each new tile through 90 degrees from the position of the last tile to ensure a more natural effect. Cut grout strip to fit as you work across the floor. Where possible, use the full length of the strip alongside multiple tiles.

Step 2

Cut tiles to fit around the edges using a utility knife and a ruler, butting the tiles right up against the wall (☛ page 75). Use Kraft paper or card templates to help shape tiles around pipes, corners and vents (☛ pages 92–93).

Step 3
When you are happy with the overall effect, tape down the entire floor with strips of painter's tape running across the room to make a large section ready for fixing with adhesive. This is a quicker and easier method than laying tiles and grout strips individually, and is possible because vinyl tiles are very light. If you want to lay tiles one by one (if you are laying a large or complex room, for example), glue them down as you would a cork floor (☞ pages 84–85).

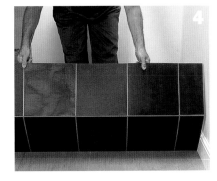

Step 4
Fold back several rows of taped-together tiles so that adhesive can be applied to the floor.

Step 5
Pour adhesive onto the floor and spread with a notched trowel, combing slightly, until the exposed section is spread to a depth of about ⅛ in. (3mm). Then replace the folded-back section of floor, pressing it down firmly onto the adhesive. Now fold the floor back from the other end of the room, until you reach the glued section. Apply adhesive to the exposed area as above, and replace the folded-back section of floor. (Replace each section within an hour, before the adhesive sets.)

Step 6
Roll the floor with a clean linoleum roller to remove air bubbles, working in all directions (press down awkward corners with your fingers). Use a damp clean cloth or sponge to wipe off adhesive that has seeped through the joints as you go. Leave to set overnight.

Step 7 (Wet areas only)
It is essential to waterproof a vinyl floor in a kitchen, bathroom or other room where water is used by sealing the gaps between the tiles and the walls with caulking. Apply the caulking with a caulking gun, and leave to dry for 24 hours.

Self-adhesive vinyl tiles
If you are using self-adhesive vinyl tiles, lay them out dry and then simply peel off the backing and stick the tiles to the floor. This method is easier than using adhesive, although you must ensure that the subfloor is completely smooth, as there will be no layer of adhesive to even out tiny imperfections. Self-adhesive tiles tend to be low-quality, and do not produce as strong a floor as tiles laid with a layer of adhesive.

THE FLOORING LAYERS

Laying on a concrete subfloor

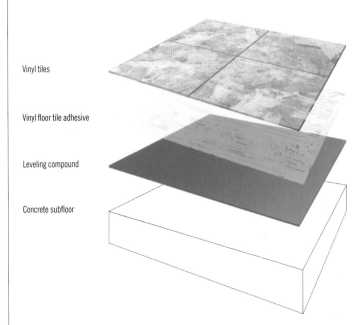

Vinyl tiles

Vinyl floor tile adhesive

Leveling compound

Concrete subfloor

Laying on a wood subfloor

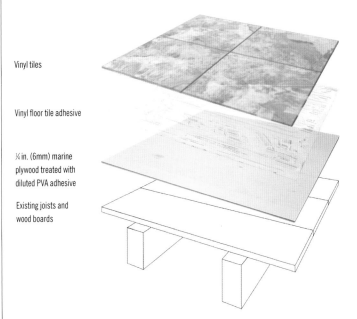

Vinyl tiles

Vinyl floor tile adhesive

¼ in. (6mm) marine plywood treated with diluted PVA adhesive

Existing joists and wood boards

INSTALLING VINYL SHEET

LEVEL OF DIFFICULTY
●●●○○

Vinyl sheet is much more difficult to handle than tiles, and fitting it around pipes, corners and vents can be tricky. If possible, you should remove moldings or baseboards before installation and replace them later.

Toolbox
1 UTILITY KNIFE AND EXTRA BLADES
2 STRAIGHTEDGE
3 PAINTER'S TAPE
4 NON-PERMANENT MARKER
5 ⅛ IN. (3MM) NOTCHED TROWEL
6 SOFT BROOM
7 CLEAN CLOTHS/SPONGES
8 CAULKING GUN (FOR WET AREAS ONLY)

Materials
9 VINYL SHEET
10 HEAVY-GRADE FELT PAPER/THICK KRAFT PAPER
11 VINYL FLOOR TILE ADHESIVE
12 CAULKING (FOR WET AREAS ONLY)

Preparing the sheet

Increase the pliability of vinyl by keeping the site warm and the sheet on site for at least 24 hours before installation. For a neater fit, remove moldings or baseboards before installation, and replace them later (☞ page 20). Cut the vinyl to size in a room that is larger than your site in order to allow yourself enough space to cut the edges.

☞ page 20

USEFUL TIP
If you are replacing vinyl sheet, and it is in good enough condition, you may be able to use the previous flooring as a template.

Step 1
Cover the perimeter of the floor (or the whole floor if you prefer) with heavy-grade felt paper or thick Kraft paper. Crease the template against the wall for a precise fit and use a utility knife to cut holes for pipes, vents and so on. If you have been unable to remove moldings, push the template under the molding as far as it will go. Attach the sheets to each other with painter's tape. To stop the template moving as you work, tape it to the floor through small slits in the paper.

Step 2
Unroll the vinyl sheet in a larger room, with the pattern side up. Overlap sheets by about 1 in. (2.5cm), and secure with painter's tape. Position the template, with the same side up as previously, on the vinyl. Line up its edges with any pattern on the vinyl, and use painter's tape to fasten it securely to the vinyl sheet through slits. Then trace the outline of the template with a non-permanent marker.

Step 3
Cut the template outline out of the vinyl using a sharp utility knife and straightedge. You will need to change blades frequently.

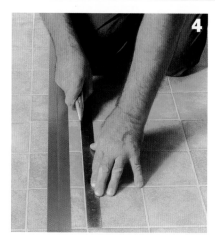

Step 4
When all the other cutting has been done, cut the joints for any overlapping sheets. Using a utility knife and straightedge, cut through both sheets simultaneously to create edges that match perfectly. You can use pattern lines as a cutting guide; alternatively, measure from the edge and join up marks with a straightedge.

Step 5
Roll up the vinyl and transport it to the site. Position it carefully. Then roll back half the sheet and pour adhesive onto the floor, spreading with a notched trowel, and combing slightly. Take care to avoid any lumps of adhesive as these will show through the thin surface of the vinyl. Continue until the exposed section is spread to a depth of around ⅛ in. (3mm).

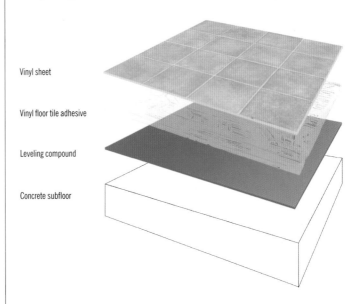

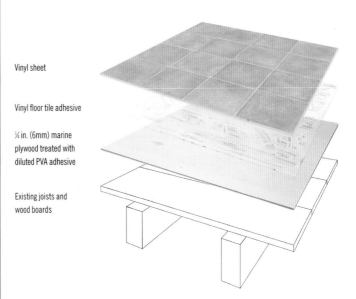

THE FLOORING LAYERS

Laying on a concrete subfloor

Vinyl sheet

Vinyl floor tile adhesive

Leveling compound

Concrete subfloor

Laying on a wood subfloor

Vinyl sheet

Vinyl floor tile adhesive

¼ in. (6mm) marine plywood treated with diluted PVA adhesive

Existing joists and wood boards

Step 7 (Areas where water is used)
A vinyl floor in a kitchen, bathroom or other room where water is used must be waterproofed by sealing the gaps between the sheet and the walls with caulking. Apply the caulking with a caulking gun, and leave to dry for 24 hours.

Step 8
Replace baseboards and moldings as necessary, gluing them to the wall or nailing them into the holes used previously.

Step 6
Ease the flooring onto the adhesive, smoothing as you go. Press down the sheet with a soft broom, working in all directions, to expel any air beneath (a linoleum roller should not be used as it might stretch the vinyl). Smooth down any awkward corners with your fingers. Wipe off adhesive that has seeped out from under the edges with a damp clean cloth. Repeat for the second half of the room, and leave the adhesive to set overnight. Wipe off any pen or pencil markings when the adhesive is dry.

Cork

PROPERTIES AT A GLANCE
(*low, **medium, ***high)
- HEAT RETENTION ***
- SOUND INSULATION ***
- LOW MAINTENANCE **
- WATER RESISTANCE **
- HARD-WEARING *

Cork is a very suitable material for flooring but sometimes ignored as an option. From an environmental standpoint, its use should certainly be encouraged. A completely natural flooring product, cork is harvested from sustainable sources, largely in Europe near the Mediterranean. Unfortunately, the increasing use of plastic corks in wine bottles is threatening some cork forests—so choosing to lay a cork floor may help their survival.

Cork is a medium-price flooring with excellent sound insulation properties, and very warm and comfortable underfoot. For these reasons, it is an interesting alternative to wood, creating a similarly friendly and natural feel in a home. Although cork is soft, dents made by dropped toys, for example, will bounce back, and it is therefore a good choice for children's rooms. However, cork is not as resistant to abrasive action as wood, linoleum or even vinyl, and won't survive as long in high-traffic areas where dirty shoes will cause scratches. The expected life of a cork floor is about 5 to 10 years, lasting longer in low-traffic areas.

Cork is favored in bathrooms because it is nonslip, as well as resilient, comfortable and warm, but the tiles must be sealed to waterproof the floor, which might otherwise absorb moisture, causing seams to swell open. You can buy ready sealed tiles but it is advisable to give even these a coat of sealant yourself once the floor is laid, to ensure that no water can penetrate the joints.

Cork is usually installed as tiles or planks. These are supplied in a variety of sizes and being light and easy to cut are simple to install (planks are laid as you would tiles). Tiles can be bought with a vinyl coating, for easy cleaning, although unlike ordinary cork these obviously lack the benefits that come from being a completely natural product.

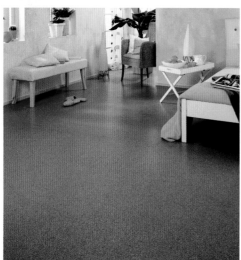

Designing the floor

Improvements in the design of vinyl and laminated floors have kicked cork out of many a bathroom and kitchen, and the colors of cork tiles—formerly available in earth tones only—have sometimes been regarded as dull. In recent years, however, some manufacturers have introduced expanded collections of colored cork flooring, covering the whole spectrum of colors, so there is now greater opportunity for creativity. Working with the new ranges, you can produce striking effects by mixing different colors in a checkerboard pattern, for example, or by using thin strips in a contrasting color to create a grouted effect.

If you want a more traditional look for your cork floor, there is also now much greater choice in subtle tones, including grays, beige and of course a wide range of browns, from honey through chestnut to mahogany. Shades of brown may be said to show the interesting grain of the cork in its best light, and certainly it is a rich brown that will best create the warm homey atmosphere for which cork is favored.

Top left: Cork is harvested only from sustainable sources, and unlike many other floors is entirely environmentally friendly.

Left: Comfortable underfoot, cork in a lively shade is a good choice for a bright bedroom.

Above: Cork in a kitchen is soft, warm and easy to clean, but be sure to seal the floor to protect the tiles from moisture.

Maintenance

Cork floors are soft and easily scratched. Sweep them gently with a soft brush, as often as possible, to remove abrasive particles of dirt that might cause damage. Wash cork floors with a sponge mop, using diluted household detergent. Wring out the mop well before use, and rinse frequently to remove grit that might otherwise scratch the floor. Your supplier will also offer various special products for cleaning and enhancing cork floors. Even prefinished cork tiles can wear out in time, so reseal them with acrylic varnish when the surface begins to look really dull (you'll notice the wear first where traffic is heaviest). Key the surface of the cork very lightly with fine-grade sandpaper before applying the varnish.

Advantages
- Soft underfoot.
- Good sound insulation.
- Very resilient.
- Particularly suitable for upstairs rooms, children's areas and bathrooms (if sealed).

Disadvantages
- Less choice of colors or patterns than is offered by other resilient floorings.
- Requires sealing (and maintenance) for waterproofing and protection from dirt.
- Less durable than other resilient flooring.

Above: The introduction of a wider range of colored tiles means that a cork floor can now be chosen to match almost any decoration scheme.

Right: Subtle earth tones show off the grain of cork in its best light and suit contemporary as well as traditional settings.

Laying a cork floor

LEVEL OF DIFFICULTY
●○○○○
Cork tiles are light, and relatively easy to cut and lay.

Before you begin laying your cork floor, remove existing floor coverings, and ensure that the subfloor is clean and smooth. Level concrete floors with leveling compound and cover wood floorboards with ¼ in. (6mm) marine plywood treated with diluted PVA adhesive (☞ pages 18–21 for detailed instructions). Make a floor plan to calculate how many tiles you need, and map out any pattern to ensure an even layout (☞ pages 12–15).

Golden rules
- Prepare the site before starting (☞ pages 18–21).
- Buy all materials at the same time to guarantee consistency and availability.
- Ask your supplier for advice, and follow the manufacturer's instructions.
- Work safely. Ventilate the room well and wear strong rubber gloves when working with adhesive, sealant or caulking.

Toolbox
1. FINE-GRADE SANDPAPER
2. CHALK LINE
3. PAINTER'S TAPE
4. UTILITY KNIFE
5. RULER
6. ⅛ IN. (3MM) NOTCHED TROWEL
7. CARPENTER'S LEVEL
8. STRAIGHTEDGE
9. CLEAN CLOTHS/SPONGES
10. LINOLEUM ROLLER
11. SOFT BROOM/ VACUUM CLEANER
12. PAINT ROLLER
13. CAULKING GUN (FOR WET AREAS ONLY)

Materials
14. CORK TILES
15. KRAFT PAPER/CARD
16. CORK FLOOR TILE ADHESIVE
17. CORK TILE SEALANT
18. CAULKING (FOR WET AREAS ONLY)

INSTALLING CORK TILES

Preparing the tiles

Cork tiles may expand or contract in response to changes in temperature and humidity. Keep the room warm and the tiles on site for at least 48 hours before installation to allow them to acclimatize. This will also increase the pliability of the cork. Before laying, sand the edges of the tiles very lightly with fine-grade sandpaper to remove any imperfections and allow the tiles to butt together properly. Then sort the tiles to harmonize any tonal variations, and stack them in piles placed conveniently around the room. Mark two chalk lines at right angles across the center of the room, to act as guides in laying out the floor, and adjust them according to the quarter method (☞ page 14). If you would like a border of contrasting tiles, start by laying out the border first (☞ page 15).

USEFUL TIP
Cork is not as durable as some flooring, so lay out the room to allow for a full-width tile in doorways, where the floor takes the most traffic.

Step 1
Lay the tiles dry along the adjusted chalk lines, fitting them closely together and holding them in place with short strips of painter's tape. Then fill in the spaces between the chalk lines, working from the center of the room toward the walls, until the entire floor except the edges is laid out in a dry run. As you work, twist each new tile 90 degrees from the position of the last tile to ensure a natural effect.

Step 2
At the room's edge, cut tiles to fit using a utility knife and a ruler, butting the tiles right up against the wall (☞ page 75). Use Kraft paper or card templates to help shape tiles around pipes, vents and corners (☞ pages 92–93).

Step 3
Once the entire floor is covered, and you are happy with the overall effect, lift a section of about 10 tiles in the corner furthest from the exit. Pour a little adhesive onto the floor and spread with a notched trowel, combing slightly. Continue until the exposed section is spread to a depth of about ⅛ in. (3mm).

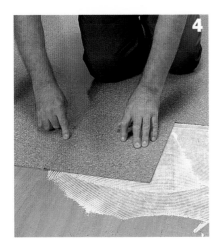

Step 4
Lay the tiles from the walls inward, working toward the exit. Make sure joints are tight, but don't slide glued tiles against each other, as adhesive may penetrate the joints and force them to bulge open. To adjust tile position, lift and re-place. Monitor the floor level as you go, using a carpenter's level (rest it on a straightedge if necessary).

Step 6
Roll the floor with a linoleum roller to remove air bubbles, working in all directions (press down awkward corners with your fingers). Wipe off adhesive that has seeped through the joints with a damp clean cloth, and leave to set overnight.

Step 7
Cork is very porous so you will need to seal the entire floor with at least one coat of cork varnish, even if you are using ready-sealed tiles, to avoid moisture working its way into the gaps and under the tiles. Sweep or vacuum the floor, then apply the sealant with a paint roller, working it over the surface of the tiles and into the joints. Mop up any excess sealant with a damp clean cloth 30 minutes after application, and leave to dry overnight.

Step 5
Lift another section of about 10 tiles, and continue in the same way until you have worked your way across the floor. Do not spread more adhesive than you can cover in an hour, as it sets quickly. Try not to kneel or walk on newly laid tiles, and wipe off surplus adhesive with a damp cloth or sponge as you go.

Step 8 (Wet areas only)
It is essential to waterproof a cork floor in a kitchen, bathroom or other room where water is used by sealing the gap between the tiles and the walls with caulking. Apply the caulking with a caulking gun, and leave to dry for 24 hours.

THE FLOORING LAYERS

Laying on a concrete subfloor

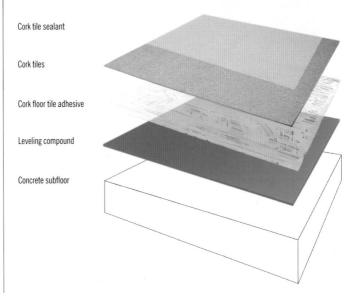

Cork tile sealant

Cork tiles

Cork floor tile adhesive

Leveling compound

Concrete subfloor

Laying on a wood subfloor

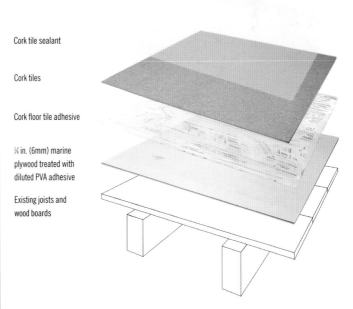

Cork tile sealant

Cork tiles

Cork floor tile adhesive

¼ in. (6mm) marine plywood treated with diluted PVA adhesive

Existing joists and wood boards

Linoleum

PROPERTIES AT A GLANCE
(*low, **medium, ***high)
- HARD-WEARING ***
- LOW MAINTENANCE ***
- HEAT RETENTION **
- SOUND INSULATION **
- WATER RESISTANCE **

The two most attractive qualities of linoleum (*true* linoleum, not vinyl) are its durability—20 years of wear is not unusual—and its composition. Linoleum is made exclusively from environmentally friendly ingredients: a blend of linseed oil, wood and cork flour, pine resin and ground limestone spread and baked over a jute backing. Unfortunately, these factors don't stop many people from associating linoleum with various mid-twentieth-century institutions, from schools to hospitals, where it was invariably the flooring of choice, often curling at the edges. Today, however, helped by an expanded range of colors and patterns as well as a desire for environmentally sustainable and less harmful products, linoleum is resurfacing as a popular flooring choice.

Linoleum is more expensive than standard vinyl, but this reflects its longer life. It shares the softness and resilience of vinyl but without its artificial feel (having thicker grades and more cushioning). Linoleum is also said to offer antibacterial and hypo-allergenic properties and, being biodegradable, it is more "green" than either vinyl or laminate. It is easy to maintain, water-resistant when properly sealed, and more burn-resistant than vinyl or laminate.

Linoleum is produced in sheet and tile form. Using tiles results in less wastage than sheet, and tiles are also much easier to install. Sheet linoleum offers the best protection against spills, but is supplied only in limited widths, so if the site is wider than about 6 ft. 6 in. (2m) you will need to seam sheets and

Designing the floor

Linoleum is a versatile flooring that is now being re-introduced in a variety of colors and design choices. It can be used to achieve a number of different looks, whether you want a sophisticated design for a contemporary hallway, retro tiles for a mid-twentieth-century kitchen, or fun, brightly colored patterns for a playroom. Colors range from soft earth tones through to bold primaries, often with a marbled finish.

Tiles in contrasting colors can be effectively used in simple designs like a classic checkerboard layout, or combined across a room in stripes. Patterned border strips are available, which you can use to edge the room or outline a patch of differently colored tiles.

Gone are the days of dreary institutional sheeting: linoleum sheet now comes in vibrant colors and exciting designs: gingham or checkerboard, for example, or even in a high-gloss mirror effect. Manufacturers offer a huge variety of features for sheeting, ranging from simple geometric motifs to coats of arms. They will even help you design a completely original floor around your own motif ideas. These feature floors are created through precise computer-assisted cutting and piecing of the sheet, and must be installed by a professional.

DECORATIVE BORDERS

FEATURE PANEL

INSET SQUARES

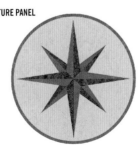

COMPASS FEATURE PANEL

waterproof the joints with a heat welder and welding rod. This technique is not recommended for amateurs, so you may need to hire a professional, or lay tiles.

Maintenance

Linoleum scratches easily, so sweep gently to remove grit. Wash the floor with a clean sponge mop, using diluted household detergent. Wring out the mop well to avoid puddles of water that may seep under the floor at the edges. Your supplier will offer various products for cleaning and enhancing linoleum floors, and for stripping residue from time to time. Linoleum achieves its true color when exposed to the light, a process known as "bloom." Patches of floor hidden under a rug, for example, may develop a yellowish cast, but this will disappear when the linoleum is exposed to the light and "blooms" again.

Advantages
- Very durable and easy to maintain.
- Environmentally friendly.
- Comfortable.
- Floors to suit a range of budgets and styles.
- Particularly suitable for kitchens, bathrooms, dining rooms, hallways and children's rooms.

Disadvantages
- More expensive than vinyl.
- Some techniques used for installing sheet are not recommended for amateurs.

Left: Linoleum is durable enough for high-traffic areas, so consider greeting visitors with a striking linoleum feature like this zig-zag pathway.

Above: Here, tiles with clipped corners, a decorative border and pretty inset tiles combine to create an atmosphere of nostalgia.

Above: Easy-to-clean and brightly colored, linoleum is a cheerful choice for family rooms.

Left: Comfortable and durable, linoleum is ideal for playrooms—so let your imagination run wild!

Above: Tiles in soft pastels arranged in a random pattern create a fresh, modern look.

Laying a linoleum floor

LEVEL OF DIFFICULTY

●●●●○

Linoleum sheet is heavier and less flexible than vinyl sheet. It is also supplied in narrower widths, so will probably need to be seamed—note that a heat welder is not recommended for use by amateurs. You may want to remove moldings or baseboards before installation.

Toolbox

1 UTILITY KNIFE AND EXTRA BLADES
2 STRAIGHTEDGE
3 PAINTER'S TAPE
4 NONPERMANENT MARKER
5 LINOLEUM KNIFE BLADES
6 HEAT WELDER
7 ⅛ IN. (3MM) NOTCHED TROWEL
8 HAIR DRYER/ PAINT STRIPPER
9 LINOLEUM ROLLER
10 CLEAN CLOTHS/SPONGES
11 HAND/AUTOMATIC ROUTER
12 CAULKING GUN (FOR WET AREAS ONLY)

Materials

13 LINOLEUM SHEET
14 HEAVY-GRADE FELT PAPER/THICK KRAFT PAPER
15 WELDING ROD
16 LINOLEUM FLOOR TILE ADHESIVE
17 CAULKING (FOR WET AREAS ONLY)

Before you begin laying your linoleum floor, remove existing floor coverings and ensure that the subfloor is clean and smooth. Level concrete floors with leveling compound and cover wood floorboards with ¼ in. (6mm) marine plywood treated with diluted PVA adhesive (☛ pages 18–21 for detailed instructions on preparing the site).

Linoleum is laid in either sheet or tiles. Tiles are easier to handle, but are more time-consuming to install in a large space. If you are installing tiles, follow the steps for laying cork tiles (☛ pages 84–85). The procedure is identical, except that linoleum should be stored on site for at least 48 hours prior to installation, whereas cork is stored on site for 24 hours.

Linoleum sheet is difficult to fit precisely and seaming requires the use of a heat welder, which is best handled by experts.

Golden rules
- **Prepare the site before starting (☛ pages 18–21).**
- **Ask your supplier for advice, and follow the manufacturer's instructions.**
- **Work safely. Wear gloves, safety glasses and a face shield when using a heat welder. Ventilate the room and wear rubber gloves when working with adhesive and caulking.**
- **Leave the adhesive to dry for at least 10 hours before using a heat welder.**

INSTALLING LINOLEUM SHEET

Preparing the sheet

Linoleum is more brittle than vinyl, and sheets may crack if they are cold. They may also expand or contract in response to changes in temperature and humidity. Keep the room warm and the flooring on site, ideally laid out flat, for at least 48 hours before installation, to allow the sheets to warm up and acclimatize. For a neater fit, remove moldings or baseboards before installation, replacing them later to hold down the edges (☛ page 20). If you are removing old sheet flooring rip it up carefully, as you may be able to use it as a template. Before cutting the linoleum to size, transport it into a room that is larger than the site you are flooring to allow yourself enough space to cut the edges.

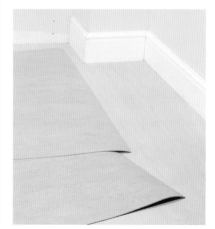

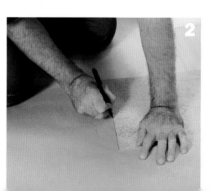

Step 1
Cover the perimeter of the floor (or the whole floor if you prefer) with heavy-grade felt paper or thick Kraft paper. Crease the template against the wall for a precise fit and use a utility knife to cut around pipes, vents and so on. If you have been unable to remove moldings, push the template under the molding as far as it will go. Attach the sheets to each other with painter's tape. To stop the template moving as you work, tape it to the floor through small slits in the paper.

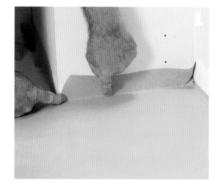

Step 3
Cut the edge outline out of the linoleum using a linoleum knife blade (which can be fitted into your utility knife). These blades are curved, and can be tricky to use with a straightedge, so you may find it easier to score with a utility knife and straightedge first. Change blades frequently.

Step 2
In a larger room, lay out the linoleum pattern side up. Overlap sheets by 1 in. (2.5cm), and secure with painter's tape. Place the template, with the same side up as previously, on the linoleum. Line up its edges with any pattern on the linoleum, and use painter's tape to fasten it to the sheet through slits. Then trace the outline of the template with a nonpermanent marker.

Step 4
When all the other cutting has been done, cut the joins for any overlapping sheets. Using a utility knife and straightedge, cut through both sheets simultaneously to create edges that match perfectly. You can use pattern lines as a cutting guide; alternatively, measure from the edge and join up marks with a straightedge.

Step 7
Use a hand or automatic router to groove the seams to the depth recommended by your supplier. Trim the welding rod (thin strips of linoleum supplied with the sheet) to the length of the joint and fuse it into the seam with a heat welder. Trim off excess with a utility knife. Leave to dry for 2 hours.

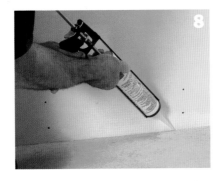

Step 5
Roll the sheet (do not fold) and transport it to the site. Position carefully. Then roll back half the flooring and pour adhesive onto the floor, spreading with a notched trowel and combing slightly. Continue until the section is spread to a depth of about ⅛ in. (3mm).

Step 8 (Areas where water is used)
It is essential to waterproof a linoleum floor in a kitchen, bathroom or other room where water is used by sealing the gap between the sheet and the walls with caulking. Apply the caulking with a caulking gun, and leave to dry for 24 hours.

Step 9
If necessary, replace baseboards and moldings, gluing them to the wall or nailing them into the holes used previously.

Step 6
Warming the sheet with a hair dryer or even a paint stripper (don't use it too close to the sheet) will make the linoleum more flexible. Ease the flooring onto the adhesive, smoothing as you go. Then roll the floor with a linoleum roller to remove air bubbles (press down awkward corners with your fingers). Wipe off adhesive that has seeped out from under the edges with a damp, clean cloth. Repeat for the second half of the room. Leave the adhesive to set for at least 10 hours (no more than 24) before using a heat welder. Remove any pen or pencil marks when the adhesive is dry.

THE FLOORING LAYERS

Laying on a concrete subfloor

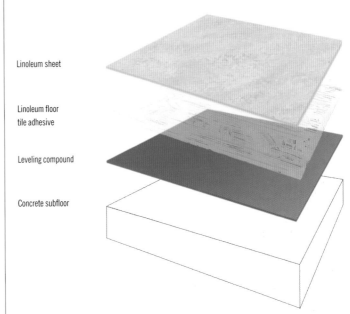

Linoleum sheet

Linoleum floor tile adhesive

Leveling compound

Concrete subfloor

Laying on a wood subfloor

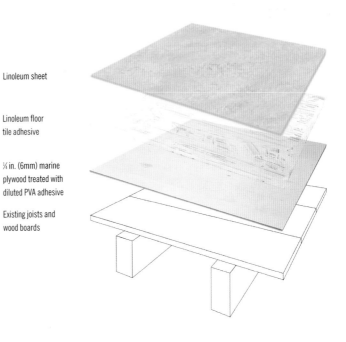

Linoleum sheet

Linoleum floor tile adhesive

¼ in. (6mm) marine plywood treated with diluted PVA adhesive

Existing joists and wood boards

Rubber

PROPERTIES AT A GLANCE
(*low, **medium, ***high)
- **HARD-WEARING** ***
- **SOUND INSULATION** ***
- **HEAT RETENTION** **
- **LOW MAINTENANCE** **
- **WATER RESISTANCE** **

Rubber flooring was originally used in industrial settings, and for a long time was available only in the most utilitarian colors. Since then, however, this flooring material has been given a complete makeover in color and design. Rubber combines a stylish, modern appearance with value for money, since a rubber floor, although expensive to buy, has an expected life of up to 20 years. Rubber also offers high resistance to cigarette and match burns, is resilient and comfortable underfoot, and absorbs sound very effectively.

Rubber flooring is available in sheet and tile form. Tiles are most frequently self-installed; sheets are best left to professional fitters. The tiles are square, and come in a variety of sizes. They are mostly synthetic; natural rubber is less durable and not often used as a flooring product. It is possible to buy environmentally friendly rubber flooring made from shredded recycled tires, but currently these are used more frequently in a public rather than a domestic context, in sports halls, for example, where shock-absorbent flooring is required.

Textured rubber has nonslip properties and this, together with its water resistance, make it an ideal flooring for bathrooms and other wet areas. Care must be taken when choosing rubber for a kitchen floor, however: grease spills represent a particular hazard, and dirt can accumulate in studded rubber textures. In other respects rubber is generally hygienic and makes for a very comfortable and warm floor.

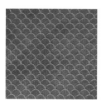
TEXTURED RELIEF

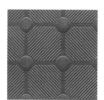
TEXTURED RELIEF

TEXTURED RELIEF

TEXTURED RELIEF

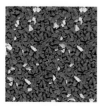
TERRAZZO EFFECT

TERRAZZO EFFECT

TERRAZZO EFFECT

MARBLED EFFECT

Designing the floor

Laying a rubber floor no longer means embracing industrial chic, although it is certainly a great choice if you want to give your home a high-tech feel (you can enhance the look by choosing metallic colors such as gray or black, and by polishing to a high sheen). Rubber is now available in a whole range of colors, from soft earth tones to startlingly bright shades, which when polished give the floor a watery gloss that is unique to rubber. Alternatively, you may prefer to leave the finish matte, for a warmer feel that complements the softness of the material. You can also buy tiles in a simulated slate, marble or terrazzo finish, or with abstract or speckled patterns that can help hide dirt and minor scratches.

Tiles may be smooth or patterned with various raised or dimpled textures, ranging from factory-look studs to designs featuring swirls or geometric shapes. As well as providing slip protection in a bathroom or other area where water is used, a studded texture adds to an industrial theme.

Consider installing a border of contrasting tiles, or creating a checkerboard or other layout to show off bold colors. If you are tiling a small space, you might even want to mix up a number of bright tiles in a random pattern across the floor!

Above: Water- and burn-resistant and very comfortable underfoot, rubber makes a practical and good-looking kitchen floor.

Maintenance

Rubber floors need regular cleaning; they tend to mark easily and solid colors quickly show the dirt. Sweep gently with a soft broom, as frequently as possible, to remove the abrasive particles of dirt that can damage the surface. Wash the floor with a sponge mop, using diluted household detergent. Keep the mop damp rather than sopping wet, and change the water regularly to avoid scratching the floor with grit. Your supplier will also offer various special products to be used for cleaning and polishing rubber floors.

Advantages
- Extremely durable.
- Water- and burn-resistant.
- Absorbs sound.
- Comfortable and warm underfoot.
- Ideal for bathrooms, kitchens, utility areas, children's rooms and anywhere a contemporary look is desired.

Disadvantages
- Expensive to buy.
- Needs regular maintenance.
- Can mark easily.

Right: The industrial aesthetic has been reinterpreted: textured rubber floors now come in a range of acid colors that when highly polished add reflective light to a setting.

Laying a rubber floor

LEVEL OF DIFFICULTY
●●○○○

Rubber tiles are more expensive, thicker and heavier than vinyl or linoleum tiles, which makes them harder to handle.

Toolbox

1 CHALK LINE
2 PAINTER'S TAPE
3 UTILITY KNIFE AND EXTRA BLADES/LINOLEUM KNIFE BLADES
4 RULER
5 SHARP SHEARS
6 ⅛ IN. (3MM) NOTCHED TROWEL
7 CARPENTER'S LEVEL
8 STRAIGHTEDGE
9 LINOLEUM ROLLER
10 CLEAN CLOTHS/SPONGES
11 SOFT BROOM/ VACUUM CLEANER
12 CAULKING GUN (FOR WET AREAS ONLY)

Materials

13 RUBBER TILES
14 KRAFT PAPER/CARD
15 RUBBER FLOOR TILE ADHESIVE
16 CAULKING (FOR WET AREAS ONLY)

Rubber tiles are laid in an almost identical way to cork or linoleum tiles, so the photographs in this section focus on more complex techniques for cutting and fitting resilient tiles.

Before you begin laying your rubber floor, remove existing floor coverings, and ensure that the subfloor is clean and smooth. Level concrete floors with leveling compound and cover wood floorboards with ¼ in. (6mm) marine plywood (☞ pages 18–21 for detailed instructions). Make a floor plan to calculate how many tiles you need, and map out any pattern to ensure an even layout (☞ pages 12–15). Rubber tiles can be thick, so buy extra blades for your utility knife and check whether you need to trim doors (☞ page 21).

Golden rules

• Prepare the site before starting (☞ pages 18–21).
• Buy all materials at the same time.
• Ask your supplier for advice, and follow the manufacturer's instructions.
• Work safely. Ventilate the room well and wear strong rubber gloves when working with adhesive and caulking.

INSTALLING RUBBER TILES

Preparing the tiles

Increase the pliability of the rubber by keeping the room warm and the tiles on site for at least 24 hours before installation. Stack them in piles placed conveniently around the room. Mark two chalk lines at right angles across the center of the room, to act as guides in laying out the floor, and adjust them according to the quarter method (☞ page 14).

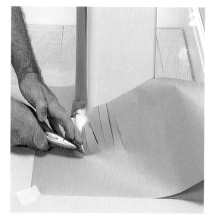

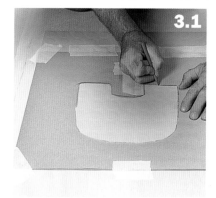

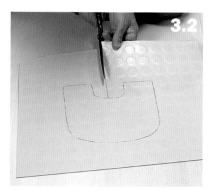

Step 1
Lay tiles dry along the adjusted chalk lines. Fit them closely together and hold them in place with short strips of painter's tape. Then fill in the spaces between the chalk lines, working from the center of the room toward the walls, until the entire floor, except the edges, is laid out in a dry run. Then cut the edge tiles using a utility knife and a ruler, butting up the tiles against the wall (☞ page 75).

Step 2
Use Kraft paper or card templates to help shape tiles around bathroom fittings such as a washbowl stand. When you reach an obstruction, cut the paper to the size of a tile and position it next to the laid tiles. Working from the wall edge of the template, slit the paper so that it can be fitted around the stand. Make further slits until the paper lies flat. Then cut off the slits, cutting around the base of the stand, to make a fitted template. Mark the position of the wall on the template.

> **USEFUL TIP**
> Rubber is hard to cut, so change blades frequently. You may want to fit a linoleum knife blade, which is curved, long and strong, into your utility knife.

Step 3
Secure the paper template with painter's tape to the tile to be cut. Trace around the inside edge of the template with a pencil, marking the outline of the fixture onto the tile below. Use a ruler to draw a line marking the wall edge of the tile, and cut along this with a utility knife. Use sharp shears to cut out the curved inside edge of the template.

RESILIENT FLOORS

Step 4
A template can also be used for cutting resilient tiles for corners. Push a square of paper into the corner gap, pressing with your fingers to form sharp creases that mark the walls. Cut out the template, and fasten it to the tile to be cut with painter's tape. Then cut along the edge of the template, using a ruler and utility knife.

Step 5
Once the entire floor is covered, and you are happy with the overall effect, lift about 10 tiles in the corner furthest from the exit. Use a notched trowel to spread adhesive over the exposed section, combing slightly, to a depth of about ⅛ in. (3mm). Work toward the exit, laying tiles with tight joints. Avoid getting adhesive into the joints and wipe up surplus adhesive as you go. Monitor the level of the floor with a carpenter's level (rest it on a straightedge if necessary). Continue until the floor is laid (☛ pages 84–85 for a pictorial guide to this sequence).

Step 6
If you are laying cut tiles that fit around fixtures, such as bathroom fittings, it can be simpler to apply adhesive directly to the underside of the tile, rather than trying to reach around the fixture.

Step 7
Roll the floor with a clean linoleum roller to remove air bubbles, working in all directions (press down awkward corners with your fingers). Wipe off adhesive that has seeped through the joints with a damp clean cloth, and leave to set overnight.

Step 8 (Areas in which water is used)
Waterproof a rubber floor in a kitchen, bathroom or other room where water is used by sealing the gap between the tiles and the walls or base of fixtures with caulking. Vacuum or sweep up any rubber dust, then apply the caulking with a caulking gun. Leave to dry for 24 hours.

THE FLOORING LAYERS

Laying on a concrete subfloor

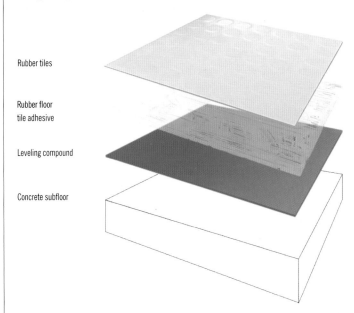

Rubber tiles

Rubber floor
tile adhesive

Leveling compound

Concrete subfloor

Laying on a wood subfloor

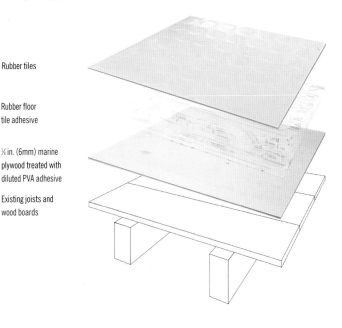

Rubber tiles

Rubber floor
tile adhesive

¼ in. (6mm) marine
plywood treated with
diluted PVA adhesive

Existing joists and
wood boards

Leather

PROPERTIES AT A GLANCE
(*low, **medium, ***high)
- **HARD-WEARING** **
- **HEAT RETENTION** **
- **LOW MAINTENANCE** **
- **SOUND INSULATION** **
- **WATER RESISTANCE** *

As flooring materials go, leather is about as natural as you can get. Warm and soft, it ages beautifully. Leather is seriously upscale, lending any space a sense of sophistication, and the combination of rich color and warmth it offers isn't found in any other type of flooring. Leather is more expensive than other resilient floorings. However, it is comparable in price to good-quality hardwood or carpet, and once installed a leather floor is surprisingly hard-wearing. It wears in slowly and over the years develops an exceptional patina. In leather, the natural wearing effects of time somehow simply add to the material's appeal. A leather floor matures with age, and for many people this lived-in look is one of its principal attractions.

Leather flooring is usually supplied in tile form. Tiles are produced as one-offs to your written requirements, usually as squares or rectangles although shapes such as hexagons or octagons can also be custom-made to suit your design ideas.

Most leather tiles are supplied prefinished, which gives them some degree of stain resistance, but despite this they must still be waxed regularly to maintain the protection. Leather and water do not mix, and so a leather floor is not suitable for installation in a kitchen, bathroom or any area with a high moisture content or where the floor may be subjected to water. Leather is a relatively expensive flooring to install, so you should invest extra time in preparing the subfloor correctly. In

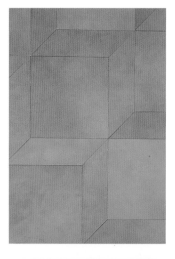
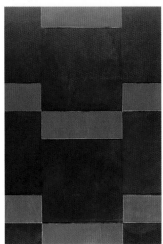
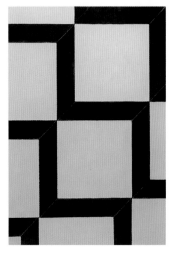

Designing the floor

Leather is usually produced in natural shades that enhance its innate beauty, with the emphasis on the luxurious richness and random variations of the material, rather than on bright colors and manufactured effects. Colors include beige, red, rust, brown, dark green and black, with the darker colors taking on an intensity that can be further enhanced by waxing to a gloss. The finish may be smooth or textured like animal hide.

There is wide scope for creativity in the shape of the tiles. As they are custom-made you can choose the size you want and even opt for a more complex shape such as a hexagon or octagon. If you request border strips or inset or key tiles in a different color you will be able to create striking geometric designs. Alternatively, you can lay a herringbone or paving design using rectangular tiles of the same color.

It is best not to attempt a very pristine look using leather, since the material scratches easily. Part of the appeal of leather is the way it ages naturally. If the floor is well cared for, with regular waxing, this ageing process will give the leather a dignity and sense of permanence that may be lacking in other resilient floors.

Left: Leather tiles are custom-made to suit your site and tastes, so discuss different options with the supplier. You may want a basketweave layout, a 3-D effect or a design that incorporates contrasting tiles of different colors, sizes or shapes

particular, it is recommended that both concrete and wood subfloors should be leveled with plywood—or the firm consistency of the leather may be ruined.

Maintenance

Leather flooring requires a little special maintenance. As with other resilient floors, it should be swept gently with a soft brush to remove abrasive particles of dirt. Never use water on leather; clean and buff it with a wax when needed (which is not very often). Your supplier will offer a range of products specific to maintaining this type of floor. Marks and scratches cannot be removed, but this natural wear and tear contributes to the beautiful patina that a leather floor develops over time.

Advantages

- Warm and soft.
- Good sound insulation.
- Looks great!
- Ideal for libraries, bedrooms, areas that benefit from sound insulation and rooms with a classy, contemporary feel.

Disadvantages

- More expensive than other resilient floors.
- Marks and scratches (but these develop into a wonderful aged patina).
- Not waterproof and therefore unsuitable for wet areas.

Right: Although traditionally supplied in somber colors such as brown and black, leather is also available in brighter shades such as leaf-green.

Below: These plain leather tiles have been laid in a basketweave pattern with an outer border of herringbone design.

Above: Burnished leather tiles in darker colors lend an intense, almost jewel-like richness to a floor.

Laying a leather floor

LEVEL OF DIFFICULTY

●●○○○

Leather is not inherently difficult to lay, but the tiles must be handled carefully as they are expensive. Do not stain them with adhesive.

Toolbox

1 CHALK LINE
2 PAINTER'S TAPE
3 UTILITY KNIFE AND EXTRA BLADES/LINOLEUM KNIFE BLADES
4 RULER
5 ⅛ IN. (3MM) NOTCHED TROWEL
6 CARPENTER'S LEVEL
7 STRAIGHTEDGE
8 CLEAN CLOTHS/SPONGES
9 LINOLEUM ROLLER
10 ELECTRIC FLOOR POLISHER (OPTIONAL)

Materials

11 LEATHER TILES
12 KRAFT PAPER/CARD
13 LEATHER FLOOR TILE ADHESIVE
14 LEATHER WAX POLISH

Before you begin the installation, remove existing coverings, and clean and level the subfloor. Leather tiles are expensive so take particular care to ensure that the subfloor is rigid and smooth, otherwise the luxurious appearance and performance of the floor will be ruined. It is recommended that you always use a layer of thick plywood under leather, so level a concrete floor or wood floorboards with ¾ in. (2cm) marine plywood treated with diluted PVA adhesive (☛ pages 18–19). Make a floor plan to calculate how many tiles you need, mapping the placement of the tiles to ensure an even layout (☛ pages 12–15).

Golden rules

• Prepare the site before starting (☛ pages 18–21), taking special care to ensure that the subfloor is rigid and level.
• Buy all materials at the same time to ensure consistency and availability.
• Ask your supplier for advice, and follow the manufacturer's instructions.
• Work safely. Ventilate the room well and wear strong rubber gloves when working with adhesive and polish.

INSTALLING LEATHER TILES

Preparing the tiles

To ease installation, increase the pliability of the leather tiles by keeping the room warm and the tiles on site for at least 24 hours before installation. Use a utility knife to scrape off any rough edges, then sort the tiles to harmonize tonal variations and stack them in piles placed conveniently around the room. Before you start, mark two chalk lines at right angles across the center of the room, to act as guides in laying out the floor, and adjust them according to the quarter method (☛ page 14). Rectangular tiles, like those shown here, look best laid in a staggered pattern. You can still use the crossed chalk lines as guides, but you will be able to lay along one axis only.

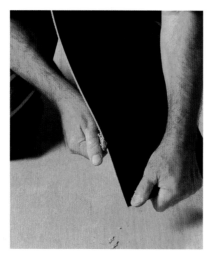

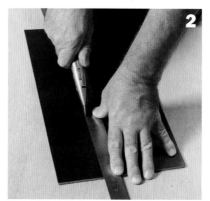

Step 1

If your tiles are square, lay them dry along the chalk cross, fitting them closely together. Rectangular leather tiles look best laid in a staggered pattern, as here. Lay along one axis of the chalk cross only, and use the other axis as a guide. Continue until the entire floor, except the edges, is laid out in a dry run.

Step 2

Cut tiles to fit around the perimeter of the room using a utility knife (fit it with a long, curved linoleum knife blade if you prefer) and a ruler (☛ page 75). Butt the tiles right up against the wall. Use Kraft paper or card templates to help shape tiles around pipes, vents and corners (☛ pages 92–93).

Step 3

Once the entire floor is covered, and you are happy with the overall effect, lift a section of about 10 tiles in the corner furthest from the exit. Pour a little adhesive onto the floor and spread with a v-notched trowel, combing slightly. Continue until the exposed section is spread to a depth of about ⅛ in. (3mm).

Step 4

Lay the tiles from the walls inward, working toward the exit. Make sure the joints are tight, but don't slide the tiles against each other, as adhesive may penetrate the joints and force them to bulge open. To adjust placement, lift and re-place tiles. Monitor the floor level as you go, using a carpenter's level (rest it on a straightedge if necessary).

Step 5

Lift another section of about 10 tiles, and continue in the same way until you have worked your way across the floor. Do not spread more adhesive than you can cover in an hour, as it sets quickly. Try not to kneel or walk on newly laid tiles. Take particular care not to spill adhesive onto the surface of the tiles, and wipe off any drips immediately with a damp cloth or sponge as you go.

Step 6

Once all the tiles are laid, roll the floor with a clean linoleum roller to remove air bubbles, working toward the edges of the room (press down awkward corners with your fingers). Wipe off adhesive that has seeped through the joints with a damp clean cloth, and leave to set overnight.

Step 7

As soon as the adhesive is dry, protect the tiles with a coat of leather wax polish, worked into the grain with a soft clean cloth. Leave to dry for 3 hours, and burnish with a soft clean cloth. Then apply 2 further coats, working as before. Allow each coat to dry before burnishing. You can use an electric floor polisher fitted with a nonabrasive pad for this procedure.

THE FLOORING LAYERS

Laying on a concrete subfloor

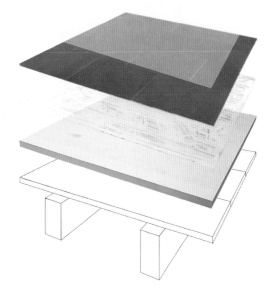

Leather wax polish

Leather tiles

Leather floor
tile adhesive

¾ in. (2cm) marine
plywood treated with
diluted PVA adhesive

Concrete subfloor

Laying on a wood subfloor

Leather wax polish

Leather tiles

Leather floor
tile adhesive

¾ in. (2cm) marine
plywood treated with
diluted PVA adhesive

Existing joists and
wood boards

WOOD FLOORS

Timelessly stylish and practical, wood remains universally popular. Choose from the palest
maple to a rich, dark walnut—or uncover the old boards hidden under your carpet and stain
them to the color of your choice. Laminate offers not only all the effects of wood at a cheaper
price, but also an increasingly realistic range of hard-floor simulations. The development of
"floating" floors, with tongues and grooves that are glued together, has brought the installation
of wood within everyone's reach, and floating laminated floors with a "click" system are even
easier to install. Solid-wood boards, however, are nailed or glued to the floor; both are difficult
procedures best attempted by professionals or experienced amateurs.

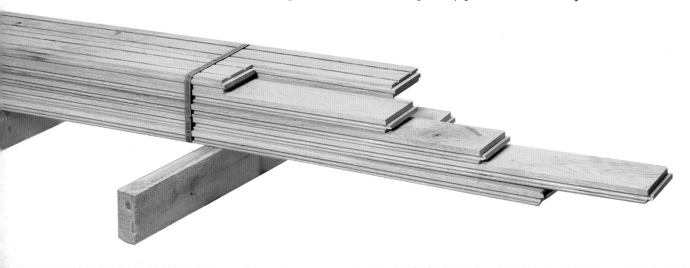

Installing wood floors

All wood and laminate floors must be protected from moisture. Even if you are laying an upper-story floor, which is less likely to be affected by moisture, it is nonetheless important to install waterproofing or risk invalidating the manufacturer's warranty. It is also essential to acclimatize wood to the conditions of the site before installation, and to leave a ½ in. (1.25cm) expansion gap around the room's edge, since all wood products expand or contract in response to changes in ambient temperature and humidity. There are three basic methods for installing a wood floor: laying a floating floor, gluing down the boards and nailing down the boards.

Floating wood or laminate floors

A floating floor is not glued or nailed to the subfloor, but held down only by baseboard moldings, furniture and the floor's own weight. The tongues and grooves of the engineered wood or laminate boards are simply glued or snapped together. This technique is easier than gluing or nailing down boards, and is the most accessible method for the inexperienced.

ENGINEERED WOOD BOARD

Glued and nailed wood floors

Solid-wood boards are now produced with tongues and grooves that slot together, but the boards are also nailed or glued to the subfloor. If you want to install solid-wood planks without tongues and grooves (if you are laying reclaimed wood, for example), the best method is to glue down the boards, butting them up tightly. Nailing and gluing wood are both challenging techniques, and not for the inexperienced.

SOLID-WOOD BOARD

How suitable is the subfloor?

Always test the subfloor for moisture (☛ page 19) before buying a wood or laminate floor, and if you find any evidence of moisture consider installing a different type of flooring. All wood floors should be underlaid with a polyethylene sheet or liquid damp-proof membrane (☛ page 19). Install waterproofing directly onto the concrete or wood subfloor. Polyethylene sheet is not recommended under glued wood floors as it would not provide a perfectly smooth or stable base for the adhesive. It is also not used under nailed wood floors, as the nails may tear the sheet and allow moisture to get through. Either polyethylene sheet or liquid damp-proof membrane can be used under wood or laminate floating floors.

Manufacturers of floating floors also recommend a foam underlayment to absorb imperfections in the subfloor and give the floor extra "bounce." You can also buy underlayments composed of foam with a waterproof backing, which combine the two underlayments in one. The sound insulation offered by these underlayments is not as effective as that provided by acoustic panels (☛ page 18). Remember to account for the effect of a raised floor level when choosing your underlayment, and ask your supplier for advice.

When laying wood or laminate it is not always necessary to level a concrete subfloor with leveling compound or to cover floorboards with marine plywood, as imperfections may be absorbed by the thickness of the floor. You can lay wood or laminate straight onto an existing wood floor, but this may make the floor too high. When installing a nailed wood floor over concrete you will always have to cover the concrete with ¾ in. (2cm) plywood in order to provide grip for the nails. Particleboard is not suitable; it does not provide enough grip.

Transition moldings

REDUCER STRIP

T-MOLDING

You may need to install a transition molding where a wood floor meets another floor, since wood is often thicker than other materials. Examples of the many types available include reducer strips, which have one sloping edge and link floors of different heights; T-moldings, which also provide a transition between floors of varying heights, with the arms of the T covering the edges of the flooring; and universal thresholds ("square nosings"), which have a steep edge and are used where wood meets carpet. Ask your supplier for guidance.

Acclimatizing wood

As any wood product, from high-density fiberboard laminate to solid-wood boards, will expand or contract in response to changes in ambient temperature and humidity, all boards must be conditioned to the climate of the site before installation. Keep the room at a normal living temperature of around 65°F (17°C) for at least a week before installation, and store the boards on site for at least 48 hours. A good way to store boards is flat on a wooden skid with a 4 in. (10cm) space underneath for ventilation.

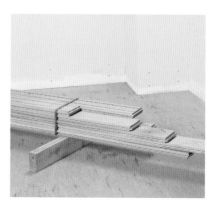

TECHNIQUES FOR WOOD FLOORS

Make a plan to calculate how wide the last board laid will be; you may need to cut the first and last boards to a similar width to avoid a very thin strip at the end. Solid-wood boards are supplied in variable lengths, so sort these before you start to ensure an even layout. For a stronger floor, plan to avoid using shorter boards in the first few rows.

An important part of designing any wood or laminate floor is planning how the joints between boards will be staggered. You should avoid siting joints side by side in adjacent boards, as this weakens the floor and creates lines that will be noticeable. The joints can be staggered in various ways.

For a more natural effect, stagger the joints randomly by at least 18 in. (46cm). This can be achieved automatically during installation, as the excess cut from the last board of a row becomes the first board of the next row.

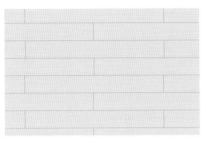

For a very regular look, perhaps in a contemporary setting, the joints can be positioned at the midpoint of adjacent boards. As a result, the joints of every other row will line up.

More regular staggered seams can be based on setting the joints two, three or four rows apart. Follow the manufacturer's instructions if in any doubt. It also helps to lay out a few trial rows to check the effect.

Expansion gaps

Ensure a consistent expansion gap of ½ in. (1.25cm), to accommodate the natural expansion and contraction of the wood, by fitting spacers between the boards and wall during installation. Spacers in a T or L shape can be bought from your wood supplier. Alternatively, cut some short lengths of wood yourself. To hide expansion gaps, remove moldings or baseboards with a cold chisel and pry bar before installation, and glue or nail them back in place afterward (☛ page 20). Baseboards are difficult to remove, so you may want to hide the expansion gap simply with an additional molding. Fasten moldings to the baseboard, not the floor, so that the boards can move.

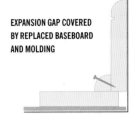

EXPANSION GAP COVERED BY REPLACED BASEBOARD AND MOLDING

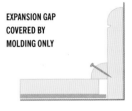

EXPANSION GAP COVERED BY MOLDING ONLY

Special tools

A tapping block is made of wood or plastic, and enables you to knock boards together with a hammer without damaging their edges. A tapping bar is made of metal, and is bent at each end so that you can "pull" boards tightly together where you don't have room to use the tapping block and hammer. Your supplier will probably provide both these items as part of the installation kit.

If you are installing a nailed wood floor, you will need a nail set, which is a punch for knocking in protruding nails. You may also want to rent an air nailer.

TAPPING BLOCK

TAPPING BAR

NAIL SET

Cutting boards

When sawing wood or laminate, wear a mask to avoid inhaling particles and work outside if possible. A fine-toothed handsaw is better for cutting than a powered jigsaw, which may tear the surface of the wood or laminate. (Saw from top to bottom to avoid splintering on the top surface.) If you require extra power, rent a portable circular saw. An electric drill with a flat wood bit may be used for drilling holes to fit around pipes. You can mark up the boards for cutting by eye, or score them using a pencil and piece of wood, as described below. A try square is useful for drawing lines at right angles.

When cutting, secure the board firmly in a clamp or similar device. With a pencil, mark a cutting line on the top side of the board, and shade the waste area. Then cut on the waste side of the line. Hold onto the waste bit as it falls away or the wood can tear.

You will most likely need to score and cut the final row of boards to fit. Lay the boards face up on top of the second-to-last row, pushing them over the gap until they reach the wall. Insert spacers between the boards and the wall to mark the expansion gap.

Hold a small piece of wood horizontally, so that it touches the wall, and in the same hand hold a pencil vertically, so that it extends down from the piece of wood to the boards. Then push the wood block slowly along the wall, tracing the cutting line with the pencil onto the boards as you go. Shade the area of each board that is to be discarded, and cut.

Wood

PROPERTIES AT A GLANCE
(*low, **medium, ***high)
- **HARD-WEARING** ***
- **HEAT RETENTION** **
- **LOW MAINTENANCE** **
- **SOUND INSULATION** *
- **WATER RESISTANCE** *

The success of laminate floors and the introduction of new quick-install systems have made wood flooring more popular than ever. Easy to clean, hard-wearing and stylish, wood is perhaps the dominant flooring material of our age. You can obtain just about every kind of wood in flooring-ready form, from popular hardwoods including maple, oak and cherry, to exotics such as merbau and iroko. The conscientious consumer should, however, insist on using only wood known to come from sustainable sources. Wood from tropical forests is less likely to be sustainably produced than are American maple, oak and cherry, all of which can be bought from certified sources. Responsible suppliers monitor their sources, and make sure of a sustainable supply by insisting on a comprehensive replanting program. Unfortunately, not all are quite as diligent as they might be. A reputable certification symbol will guarantee the source to be environmentally trustworthy, so if in doubt, ask to see the supplier's certificate for the wood concerned. The Forest Stewardship Council (FSC) is an example of a nonprofit organization, set up to monitor forest management, that certifies suppliers of wood from sustainable sources (☛ www.fscus.org for more information). If you want to be really green, track down reclaimed wood flooring, which

OAK

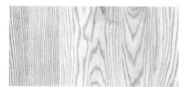

BEECH

ASH

MAPLE

CHERRY

WALNUT

Designing the floor

Different woods have different properties, including a distinctive color and grain; pale maple, for example, will give a room a very different feel to one laid with rich red-brown cherry. Hardwoods vary a little in price, with walnut one of the most expensive and beech among the cheapest; only pine, as a softwood, is considerably cheaper. Different grades of wood are also available at different costs: the most expensive will be very evenly colored with few knots. All hardwoods are tough enough for domestic use, although some, such as maple, are tougher than others. Here are some of the most popular types of wood used in flooring:

Right: The rich, deep tones of cherry create a sophisticated high-status floor that would work equally well in a modern or traditional setting.

Walnut
Walnut is probably the most popular dark hardwood for flooring, although it is much softer than oak, maple or cherry. It has a lovely deep brown color.

Cherry
This hardwood has a delicious red-brown color that darkens with age, and an interesting wavy grain.

Oak
Oak is a very tough hardwood, with a mid-brown color, and is the most popular hardwood flooring used in North America. Grayish white oak has a straight, consistent grain; red oak has more patterning and suits a rustic setting.

is usually of high quality although it may require repair such as removing nails, sanding, planing and revarnishing. You might also consider bamboo, which is a grass rather than a tree and grows back very quickly when harvested.

Hardwood is more durable than softwood and available in a wider range of colors and grain patterns. Unfortunately, hardwood is also much more expensive than softwood, which is one reason why laminated floors have become so popular, since they offer all the visual effect of hardwood together with ease of installation at a fraction of the cost. If you are considering installing wood, first check under your present flooring to see if there are floorboards already there. Unless your house is very old, these boards are likely to be softwood of varying quality

Advantages
- Very durable and easy to clean.
- Gives a warm and natural effect.
- Looks good in homes of any age.
- Particularly suitable for living rooms, dens, hallways and stairs.

Disadvantages
- Can be noisy if not sound insulated.
- Dusty and drafty if laid directly onto joists.
- Not ideal for wet areas like bathrooms.

Left: Its subtlety and smoothness allow beech to work well in an airy modern setting.

Below right: There's nothing quite like a floor that's been there for years. You can stain oak boards to replicate the patina of age, and create a wonderfully traditional atmosphere.

Fir
Colors range from pale yellow to light red and often become warmer when exposed to sunlight. Fir is softer than other hardwoods and therefore usually used in areas of low traffic.

Ash
Ash has a distinctive, open grain that starts out pale but deepens over time. It can be pickled (bleached) or stained for an interesting effect that defines the grain.

Beech
This is a mid-brown to pinkish-white hardwood with a flecked grain. Beech is consistent in tone and patterning, so fits well into a contemporary context. It is also ideal for staining.

Bamboo
Bamboo flooring is supplied as prefinished engineered boards rather than solid planks. The striped grain of bamboo yields an intriguing effect, in a dark or light finish. Bamboo combines an exotic appeal with environmentally friendly credentials.

Birch
Pale in color, with a straight, closed grain, birch lends a light, airy feel to a room. This wood is softer than hardwoods such as oak.

Pine
Most eighteenth and nineteenth-century wood floorboards were made from pine. It is the most widely used softwood flooring and is naturally pale, though can be antiqued with stain and will take on a warm hue with age.

Maple
This hardwood is pale, with a very fine grain pattern. Ideal for a modern setting, maple is a sophisticated and very durable wood.

and consistency, and are generally considered a subfloor. Some old softwood boards can be sanded and polished to a beautiful finish. Others may need some repair first. Modern floorboards found under a carpet, however, may be too insubstantial to be used as anything more than a subfloor. The most economical option if you decide to install a completely new wood floor is to use softwood instead of hardwood, finishing it by painting or staining. Remember that softwoods are relatively easily dented and should not be laid in high-traffic areas such as entrances and stairways.

If you choose to install a new wood floor, you must decide on the form of wood you want: engineered board, solid board or wood tile. Your choice will dictate the method you use to install the floor: laying a floating floor, or gluing or nailing down the wood. Engineered boards are the most popular choice for new floors and are laid as a floating floor. This is the easiest wood installation method, with the floor held down simply by baseboards, furniture and its own weight.

Wood floors are finished in various ways, such as clear or stain varnishing, oiling, waxing, painting or pickling (bleaching).

Above: All laminate boards, and an increasing number of engineered wood boards, have a "click" system, whereby tongues and grooves are simply slotted together without the need for glue.

Types of wood board

You can buy wood floors as solid-wood boards, as manufactured boards consisting of a hardwood veneer on a softwood base (engineered boards) and as wood tiles. Jointing methods range from simple square edges, to tongue and groove, to sophisticated joints that snap together.

Engineered wood boards

These prefinished boards are laid as a floating floor. They are manufactured by attaching a hardwood layer to a softwood base, often with a very thin plywood bottom layer to improve moisture resistance and stability. The top, hardwood layer is made from one, two or three strips, with the one-strip version being known as plank. The boards are usually supplied with tongued-and-grooved edges for gluing together. Some engineered wood boards now use the laminate "click" system, in which tongues and grooves are simply clicked together. Another version of the engineered board has a high-density base and a very thin wood veneer; it is cheaper than other engineered wood boards, but more expensive than laminate and less durable than other wood boards.

Engineered wood boards are usually prefinished with five to eight coats of oxide lacquer baked into the surface, and need no further finishing. They are lighter than solid wood boards, and laying a floating floor is less difficult than the glue- or nail-down methods. Another advantage is that the plywood base makes the boards less prone than solid wood to expansion and contraction after installation, although you will still need to leave expansion gaps around the room.

Solid wood boards

These are usually supplied in random lengths, with tongue-and-groove edges for gluing or nailing. (Straight-edged solid-wood boards, normally reclaimed wood, are butted up closely and glued to the subfloor.) Solid boards are often unfinished, in which case you will need to finish them yourself after installation, using varnish, oil or wax. The boards are sometimes laminated together to form two- or three-strip-wide planks, which are treated as solid single-strip boards (and should not be confused with engineered boards where the veneer surface has a strip-board pattern). Made of solid wood, these boards are heavier than engineered boards, and nailing or gluing them down is much more difficult than laying a floating wood floor. Solid wood boards are also more prone to expansion and contraction after installation.

Wood tile (parquet)

This product is sometimes called parquet or wood mosaic. Wood "tiles" are thin strips of wood arranged in various patterns, such as herringbone, and glued to a square of plywood or MDF. To install the tiles, glue them to the subfloor as you would lay tiles such as cork. "Self-stick" tiles are also available. Originally these patterns would have been created with individually laid wood blocks, and were a true art. Original parquet floors are undoubtedly worth restoring, but today the look of parquet is replicated with these ready-manufactured tiles, which are easier to install and more affordable than real parquet.

Left: The flamboyant grain and lively colors of an ash floor make it perfect for a contemporary setting.

Right: There are a range of quick-install systems on the market: talk to your supplier to find the wood floor that's right for you.

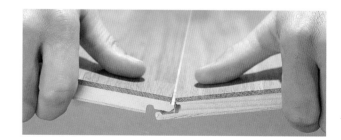

These methods can all be used to make cheaper wood look more expensive or to give an existing surface new impact.

Maintenance

Sweep the floor with a soft broom to remove abrasive particles of dirt that may damage the finish. You can wash wood with a clean sponge mop, using diluted household detergent, so long as you wring the mop well before use. Routinely mop up spills immediately to avoid the wood being damaged by moisture. Your supplier will also offer various special cleaning products that are applied either in a spray or with a mop, and wiped off when dry (remember that these are not always necessary). Wood floors supplied to you unfinished need more care than prefinished boards. Any finish that you have applied yourself won't last as long as the many coats of sealer baked onto prefinished boards, and further coats will be needed every six months. You'll know it's time to reseal when the floor starts to look dull, or water soaks into the wood rather than remaining on the surface of the floor.

Top left: Laying traditional parquet is a difficult technique best left to skilled craftsmen. It is well worth restoring an old parquet floor; alternatively the look can be simulated through wood tiles.

Left: Maple is renowned for its sleek appearance and resistance to wear.

Above: Pale Scandinavian woods can offer the luxurious effect of white carpeting combined with durability and ease of maintenance.

Laying a floating wood floor

LEVEL OF DIFFICULTY

●●●○○

Also called an engineered floor, this is the easiest wood floor for nonprofessionals to install, as it is held down only by base moldings, furniture and its own weight.

Toolbox

1 UTILITY KNIFE/SHEARS
2 DUCT TAPE
3 CHALK LINE
4 TRY SQUARE
5 STRAIGHTEDGE
6 ½ IN. (1.25CM) SPACERS
7 HAMMER
8 TAPPING BLOCK
9 CLEAN CLOTHS (LIKE CHEESECLOTH)
10 FINE-TOOTH HANDSAW/ PORTABLE CIRCULAR SAW
11 ELECTRIC DRILL WITH WOOD BIT
12 TAPPING BAR

Materials

13 ENGINEERED WOOD BOARDS
14 WATERPROOFED FOAM UNDERLAYMENT
15 WOOD ADHESIVE
16 MATCHING WOOD FILLER
17 MATCHING MOLDINGS AND BASEBOARDS (IF DESIRED)
18 MINERAL SPIRITS

A floating floor may be laid straight onto existing boards, and leveling with plywood is only necessary if the boards are in bad condition. Similarly, use leveling compound only if a concrete subfloor is very uneven (☛ pages 18–19). Check if you need to trim doors (☛ page 21). If you can, remove vent grills, as well as moldings and baseboards (☛ page 20), which will be replaced later to hide the expansion gap. Always install a damp-proof membrane and a cushioning foam underlayment. You can also buy combined underlayment composed of foam with a waterproof backing. Ask your supplier for the recommended underlayment and adhesive for your type of wood floor. You should make a floor plan to establish how many boards you need, and how wide the first and last rows should be.

The engineered boards used for floating wood floors are usually prestained and prevarnished, and therefore will probably not need staining or sealing. Most are installed by gluing tongues and grooves, but glueless floating wood floors are also available. If you want to lay boards with a glueless "click" system, follow the step-by-step instructions to installing a floating laminated floor (☛ pages 120–121).

Golden rules

- Prepare the site before starting (☛ page 18–21).
- Ask your supplier for advice, and follow the manufacturer's instructions.
- Work safely. Ventilate the room and wear rubber gloves when working with adhesive. When sawing, clamp boards and wear a mask to avoid inhaling dust. Wear a mask, safety glasses, gloves and ear protection when using power tools.
- Always check the site for moisture and underlay wood floors with damp-proofing (☛ page 19). If moisture is present, consider laying a more water-resistant flooring.

INSTALLING ENGINEERED WOOD BOARDS

Preparing the boards

Wood may expand or contract in response to changes in temperature and humidity. Keep the room warm and acclimatize the flooring by storing it on site for at least 48 hours before installation. Before you start, you may want to lay a few test rows to check the look of the staggered jointing. To establish a straight start line in Step 2, snap a chalk line along the longest and straightest wall, at a distance of the width of the first board, plus the width of the tongue (usually 1 in. or 2.5cm), plus an expansion gap of ½ in. (1.25cm). You may want to saw off the tongues from the first row of boards, in which case do not account for these when measuring. If the wall is not straight, use a try square to establish a straight line at the correct distance from a corner. Extend this line along the floor with a straightedge, and use it as a guide when snapping the chalk line. Gaps caused by uneven walls can be filled later with wood filler or boards cut lengthwise, or covered by moldings.

Step 1

Before laying the boards, cover the floor with a combined underlayment composed of foam with a waterproof backing. Cut to fit using a utility knife and shears, then butt up the pieces and join them with duct tape. Alternatively, install a layer of polyethylene waterproof sheet or liquid damp-proof membrane, followed by a layer of foam underlayment, as shown in *Laying a laminated floor* (☛ page 120). Unless a wood subfloor is very damaged, you will not need to level it with plywood. If plywood is necessary, install it over the waterproofing (☛ page 18).

Step 2

Snap a chalk line marking the outer edge of what will be the first row of boards, as described above (*Preparing the boards*). Lay the first board against the chalk line, with its tongued edge toward the walls (saw off the tongues for a neater fit). Fit ½ in. (1.25cm) spacers between the board and the wall to ensure a consistent expansion gap.

Step 3

Apply a bead of glue to the tongue at the end of the next board, and lower it to the floor at an angle, inserting the tongue into the groove of the laid board. Use a hammer and tapping block to knock the board gently into place. Then continue along the row, fitting spacers between the boards and the wall as you work. Wipe off surplus adhesive immediately with a damp, clean cloth.

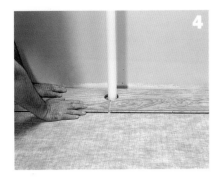

THE FLOORING LAYERS

Laying on a concrete subfloor

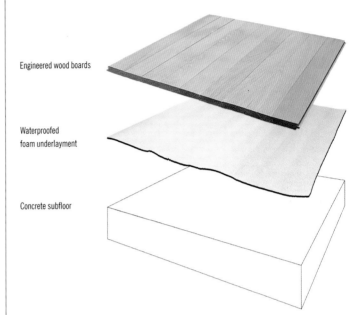

Engineered wood boards

Waterproofed
foam underlayment

Concrete subfloor

Step 4
When you reach the end of the row, cut the last board to fit (☛ page 101), allowing for a ½ in. (1.25cm) expansion gap. Draw true lines with a try square, and cut with a fine-tooth handsaw or portable circular saw. Saw from top to bottom to avoid splintering the top surface. Use the electric drill to drill holes for pipes and other obstacles.

Step 6
If you have trimmed the door jamb, gently knock a board under the jamb with a tapping block and hammer. You may need to saw off a corner of the board to fit around the wall. When you reach the final row, cut the boards lengthwise to fit (☛ page 101), allowing for a ½ in. (1.25cm) expansion gap. Pull in the last row tightly with a tapping bar, inserting spacers between the boards and wall to hold the row in place (as demonstrated in *Laying a laminated floor*, ☛ page 121). Cut boards to fill any large gaps caused by uneven walls.

Laying on a wood subfloor

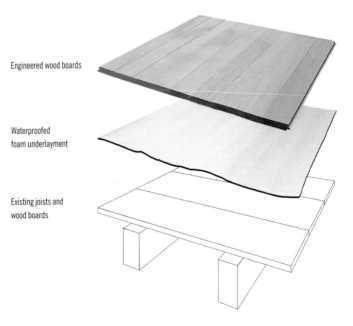

Engineered wood boards

Waterproofed
foam underlayment

Existing joists and
wood boards

Step 5
Use the balance of the cut board, laid with the cut edge toward the wall, to start the second row. This will ensure board joints in adjacent rows are staggered for rigidity and appearance. Stagger joints by at least 18 in. (46cm). Continue to lay the floor, gluing tongues and fitting them into grooves. Knock each board gently home with a hammer and tapping block. If you make a mistake, pull the boards apart before the adhesive sets.

Step 7
Leave the adhesive to set overnight, then remove the spacers. Remove any residue of adhesive with a clean cloth and a little mineral spirits. Fill small gaps with matching wood filler. Wipe off any excess filler with a damp clean cloth, and leave to dry for about an hour.

Step 8
Reinstall moldings, baseboards and vents to cover the expansion gaps and any small gaps caused by uneven walls.

Laying a glued solid-wood floor

LEVEL OF DIFFICULTY
●●●●○

This type of flooring is difficult to install because adhesive sets quickly and the heavy solid-wood boards are difficult to maneuver. Boards may also easily be nudged out of position during the installation process.

Toolbox
1. PAINT ROLLER
2. CHALK LINE (WITH COLORED CHALK)
3. TRY SQUARE
4. STRAIGHTEDGE
5. ⅛ IN. (3MM) NOTCHED TROWEL
6. CLEAN CLOTHS (SUCH AS CHEESECLOTH)
7. ½ IN. (1.25CM) SPACERS
8. PAINTER'S TAPE
9. FINE-TOOTH HANDSAW/ PORTABLE CIRCULAR SAW
10. ELECTRIC DRILL WITH WOOD BIT
11. HAMMER
12. TAPPING BLOCK
13. TAPPING BAR

Materials
14. SOLID-WOOD BOARDS
15. LIQUID DAMP-PROOF MEMBRANE
16. WOOD ADHESIVE
17. MATCHING WOOD FILLER
18. MINERAL SPIRITS
19. MATCHING MOLDINGS AND BASEBOARDS (IF DESIRED)

A glued wood floor may be laid onto existing floorboards, and leveling with marine plywood treated with diluted PVA adhesive is only necessary if they are in bad condition. Similarly, you only need to level a concrete subfloor with leveling compound if the surface is very uneven (☛ pages 18–19). Check if you have to trim doors to accommodate the new floor height (☛ page 21). If you can, remove vent grills, as well as moldings and baseboards (☛ page 20), which will be replaced later to hide the expansion gap (or you can install new moldings and baseboards that match the floor). You should also make a floor plan to establish how many boards you need, and how wide the first and last rows should be.

Glued wood floors must be underlaid with a liquid damp-proof membrane painted onto the concrete or the wood subfloor. Polyethylene sheet is not recommended for use as waterproofing as it would provide an unstable base for the glue. Check with your supplier about the recommended underlayment and adhesive for the type of floor you are laying.

Solid-wood boards are supplied in a variety of woods, finished and unfinished. If you want to stain, pickle (bleach) or seal unfinished boards yourself, follow the step-by-step instructions to finishing a wood floor (☛ pages 114–115), once the floor is in place.

Golden rules
- Prepare the site before starting (☛ pages 18–21).
- Ask your supplier for advice, and follow the manufacturer's instructions.
- Work safely. Ventilate the room well and wear strong rubber gloves when working with adhesive. Clamp boards firmly when sawing and wear a mask to avoid inhaling dust. Wear a mask, safety glasses, gloves and ear protection when using power tools.
- Always check the site for moisture and underlay wood floors with waterproofing (☛ page 19). If moisture is present, consider laying a more water-resistant flooring.

INSTALLING SOLID-WOOD BOARDS WITH GLUE

Preparing the boards

Wood expands or contracts in response to ambient temperature and humidity. To acclimatize the flooring, keep the room warm and store the flooring on site for at least 48 hours before installation. Solid-wood boards are supplied in varying lengths, so sort them before you start and lay a few trial rows to check the effect of the joint staggering. Different lengths of board should be evenly distributed across the room, but avoid using the shortest lengths in the first few rows as this may weaken the floor.

To establish a straight start line in Step 2, snap a chalk line along the longest and straightest wall, at a distance of the width of the first board, plus the width of the tongue (usually 1 in. or 2.5cm), plus an expansion gap of ½ in. (1.25cm). Use colored chalk to ensure the line is visible through the adhesive. If the wall is not straight, use a try square to establish a straight line at the correct distance from a corner. Extend this line along the floor with a straightedge, and use it as a guide when snapping the chalk line. Gaps caused by uneven walls can be filled later with wood filler or boards cut lengthwise, or covered by moldings.

Step 1
Paint liquid DPM onto the subfloor. (A layer of plywood is not usually needed; if it is, install on top of the waterproofing, ☛ page 18.) Leave to dry for at least two hours.

Step 2
Snap a chalk line marking the outer edge of what will be the first row of boards, as described above (*Preparing the boards*). Pour a little adhesive onto the floor where the first row of boards will be laid. Start ½ in. (1.25cm) from the wall, spreading with a notched trowel to a depth of ⅛ in. (3mm), until the whole area up to the chalk line is covered. Lay the first board against the chalk line, with its tongued edge toward the wall, and press it firmly into the adhesive. Fit ½ in. (1.25cm) spacers between the board and wall to ensure a consistent expansion gap.

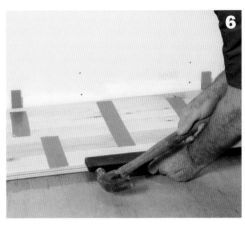

Step 3

Apply a bead of glue to the tongue at the end of your second board. Lower it to the floor at an angle, fitting its tongue into the groove of the laid board, and press it firmly into the layer of adhesive. Then continue along the row, fitting spacers between the boards and the wall as you work. Wipe off surplus adhesive immediately with a damp, clean cloth.

USEFUL TIP
Tape boards together with painter's tape to stop them moving during fitting (remove the tape within 24 hours to avoid marking the wood).

Step 4

When you reach the end of the row, cut the last board to fit (☞ page 101), allowing for a ½ in. (1.25cm) expansion gap. Draw true lines with a try square, and cut with a fine-tooth handsaw or portable circular saw. Saw from top to bottom to avoid splintering the top surface. Use an electric drill with wood bit to drill holes for pipes. When the whole row is laid, allow the adhesive to set for an hour to provide a firm edge to push against while laying other rows.

Step 5

Use the balance of the cut board, laid with the cut edge toward the wall, to start the second row. This ensures that board joints in adjacent rows are staggered for rigidity and effect. Stagger joints by at least 18 in. (46cm). Continue laying the floor as above, spreading adhesive for only one row at a time, and gluing tongues and fitting them into the grooves of the laid boards. You do not need to leave each row to dry for an hour, but do not walk on the laid boards.

Step 6

After you have installed a few rows, use a tapping block and hammer to gently knock the boards together and close the seams. Continue using the tapping block and hammer to tighten joints as you work.

Step 7

Cut the boards in the final row lengthwise to fit (☞ page 101), remembering to allow for a ½ in. (1.25cm) expansion gap. Lay these boards with adhesive, as above. Use a tapping bar to pull in the last row tightly, inserting spacers to hold it in place. Cut boards to fill large gaps caused by uneven walls.

Step 8
Leave the adhesive to set overnight, then remove the spacers. Remove any residue adhesive with a clean cloth and a little mineral spirits. Fill small gaps with matching wood filler. Wipe off any excess with a damp clean cloth, and leave to dry for about an hour.

Step 9
Replace vent grills, and reinstall baseboards and moldings to cover expansion gaps and any unevenness caused by walls that are not perfectly straight.

THE FLOORING LAYERS

Laying on a concrete subfloor

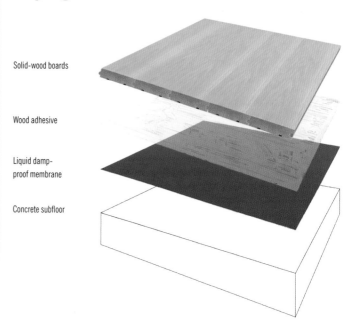

Solid-wood boards

Wood adhesive

Liquid damp-proof membrane

Concrete subfloor

Laying a patterned wood floor

A traditional parquet floor is very difficult to install and is usually undertaken only by an experienced craftsperson. In this technique, short blocks of solid wood are individually glued to the subfloor, creating a pattern such as herringbone. You can, however, buy panels of wood ready-glued into parquet patterns, which are much easier to fit. These panels (essentially tiles) can be installed following the step-by-step instructions for laying cork tiles (☞ pages 84–85), using the adhesive recommended by your supplier. Wood tiles are not always prefinished, so they may need sealing (☞ pages 114–115).

Laying on a wood subfloor

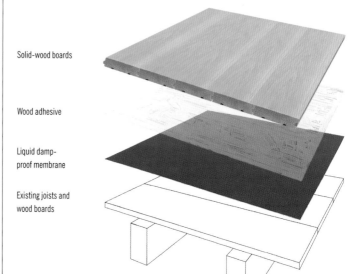

Solid-wood boards

Wood adhesive

Liquid damp-proof membrane

Existing joists and wood boards

Laying a nailed solid-wood floor

LEVEL OF DIFFICULTY

●●●●○

This type of flooring is tricky to install because of the amount of nailing involved, and also because the heavy solid-wood boards are very difficult to maneuver.

Toolbox

1 PAINT ROLLER
2 CHALK LINE
3 TRY SQUARE
4 STRAIGHTEDGE
5 ½ IN. (1.25CM) SPACERS
6 ELECTRIC DRILL WITH WOOD BIT
7 HAMMER AND NAILS
8 AIR NAILER (OPTIONAL)
9 TAPPING BLOCK
10 NAIL SET
11 FINE-TOOTH HANDSAW/PORTABLE CIRCULAR SAW
12 ⅛ IN. (3MM) NOTCHED TROWEL
13 TAPPING BAR
14 CLEAN CLOTHS (SUCH AS CHEESECLOTH)

Materials

15 SOLID-WOOD BOARDS
16 LIQUID DAMP-PROOF MEMBRANE
17 WOOD ADHESIVE
18 MATCHING WOOD FILLER
19 MATCHING MOLDINGS AND BASEBOARDS (IF DESIRED)

A nailed wood floor can be installed onto existing floorboards, and leveling with marine plywood is only necessary if these are in bad condition. Concrete subfloors, however, must be covered with ¾ in. (2cm) marine plywood (☛ page 18) to provide grip for the nails (particleboard is not suitable). You do not need to use leveling compound unless the concrete is very uneven. You may need to trim doors to the new floor height (☛ page 21). If you can, remove vent grills, as well as moldings and baseboards (☛ page 20), which will be replaced later to hide the expansion gap (or install new matching moldings and baseboards). You should make a plan of the floor to establish how many boards you need and how wide the first and last rows should be.

Nailed wood floors must be underlaid with a liquid damp-proof membrane, painted onto the concrete or the wood floorboards. Polyethylene sheet is not recommended, as the nails may pierce the sheeting. Check with your supplier about the recommended underlayment and adhesive for your floor.

If you want to stain, pickle (bleach) or seal unfinished solid-wood boards yourself, follow the step-by-step instructions to finishing a wood floor (☛ pages 114–115) once the floor is in place.

Golden rules

• **Prepare the site before starting** (☛ pages 18–21).
• **Ask your supplier for advice, and follow the manufacturer's instructions.**
• **Work safely.** Ventilate the room well and wear strong rubber gloves when working with adhesive. Clamp boards firmly when sawing and wear a mask to avoid inhaling dust. Wear a mask, safety glasses, gloves and ear protection when using power tools.
• **Always check the site for moisture and underlay wood floors with waterproofing** (☛ page 19). If moisture is present, consider laying a more water-resistant flooring.

INSTALLING SOLID WOOD BOARDS WITH NAILS

Preparing the boards

Wood expands and contracts in response to changes in ambient temperature and humidity. To acclimatize the flooring, keep the room warm and store the flooring on site for at least 48 hours before installation. Solid-wood boards are supplied in varying lengths, so sort them before you start, bearing in mind how you would like the joints to be staggered. Lay a few trial rows to check the effect. Different lengths should be evenly distributed across the room, but avoid using the shortest lengths in the first few rows as this may weaken the floor. Any gaps around the edges caused by uneven walls can be filled later with wood filler or boards cut lengthwise, or covered by moldings.

Pre-drill holes at 6 in. (15cm) intervals along the grooved edge of what will be the first row of boards. All nailing after the first row will be through the tongues only, so that it is not visible.

Step 1
Vacuum or sweep the subfloor thoroughly. Use a paint roller to paint the subfloor with a coat of liquid damp-proof membrane, and leave to dry for about 2 hours. Unless a wood subfloor is very damaged, you will not need to level it with plywood (if plywood is necessary, install this over the waterproofing). If your subfloor is concrete, glue down ¾ in. (2cm) marine plywood, over the waterproofing, to provide grip for the nails (☛ pages 18–19).

Step 2
Snap a chalk line along the longest and straightest wall, at a distance of ½ in. (1.25cm). If the wall is not straight, use a try square to establish a straight line at the correct distance from a corner. Extend this line along the floor with a straightedge and use it as a guide when snapping the chalk line. Lay the first board along the chalk line, with its grooved edge toward the wall. Fit ½ in. (1.25cm) spacers to ensure a consistent expansion gap between the board and the wall. Then hammer in nails through the pre-drilled holes along the grooved wall edge.

Step 3

Drill holes at an angle of 45 degrees, at 6 in. (15cm) intervals, through the tongue along the side facing the center of the room. Then hammer nails through the tongue and into the subfloor. Using an air nailer is a quicker method, but can be dangerous.

Step 4

Lay the second board, slotting it in the end of the first board, and knocking it gently into place with a tapping block and hammer. As before, nail through the pre-drilled holes next to the wall, and also drill holes in the tongue and nail through these. Then continue working along the row, punching in protruding nails with a nail set and hammer.

Step 5

When you reach the end of the row, cut the last board to fit (☛ page 101), allowing for a ½ in. (1.25cm) expansion gap. Draw true lines with a try square, and cut with a fine-tooth handsaw or portable circular saw. Saw from top to bottom to avoid splintering the top surface. Use the electric drill to drill holes for pipes and other obstacles.

Step 6

Use the balance of the cut board, laid with the cut edge toward the wall, to start the second row. This will ensure board joints in adjacent rows are staggered for rigidity and effect. Use a tapping block and hammer to knock the new board gently onto the protruding tongue of the board in the previous row. Then drill holes in the tongue and nail the board to the floor (alternatively, use an air nailer).

Step 7

Continue to work across the floor, staggering joints by at least 18 in. (46cm). Use a tapping block and hammer to knock tongues and grooves into place, and secure the boards by nailing through the tongues, as before.

Step 8

Do not nail down the second-to-last row until you have cut the boards in the final row lengthwise to fit (☛ page 101), remembering to allow for a ½ in. (1.25cm) expansion gap. The last two rows will be laid as one. Glue the boards of the last two rows together using wood adhesive, and set aside for an hour to set.

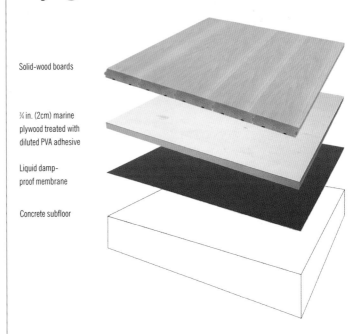

THE FLOORING LAYERS

Laying on a concrete subfloor

Solid-wood boards

¾ in. (2cm) marine plywood treated with diluted PVA adhesive

Liquid damp-proof membrane

Concrete subfloor

Laying on a wood subfloor

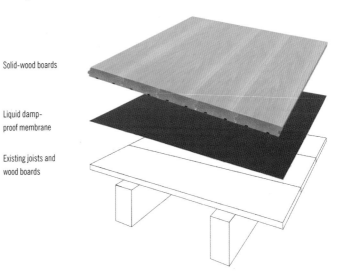

Solid-wood boards

Liquid damp-proof membrane

Existing joists and wood boards

Step 9
You will have to glue down the last (double) row of boards as you will not be able to reach the tongues with the drill or air nailer. Use a notched trowel to spread a layer of adhesive along what will be the last row, to a depth of about ⅛ in. (3mm).

Step 10
Press the boards firmly into the adhesive as you lay them and use a tapping bar to pull in the row tightly, inserting spacers to hold boards in place. Leave the adhesive to set overnight before walking on this part of the floor. If there are any large gaps caused by uneven walls, cut boards lengthwise to fit and glue them to the subfloor.

Step 11
Remove all spacers. Fill small gaps with matching wood filler. Wipe off excess filler with a damp clean cloth, and leave to dry for at least an hour.

Step 12
Replace vents, and reinstall baseboards and moldings to cover expansion gaps and any small gaps caused by uneven walls.

Finishing a wood floor

WARNING
SAWDUST AND SEALANT-SOAKED CLOTH ARE BOTH HIGHLY FLAMMABLE AND MUST BE DISPOSED OF ACCORDING TO LOCAL SAFETY REGULATIONS.

Although all engineered boards and many solid-wood planks are supplied prestained and prefinished, you may decide to install unfinished wood planks, and finish the floor yourself. Alternatively, you may want to sand down an existing wood floor and apply a new finish of your choice. You can alter or enhance the appearance of wood through staining, pickling (bleaching), color varnishing or painting, and you will need to protect an untreated floor by sealing it with varnish, oil or wax.

Prevarnished engineered boards do not need to be sealed. Manufacturers will offer a brand-name polish for maintenance, and also matching wood filler to plug gaps and cracks. Apply filler to the gap, wipe off any surplus with a damp cloth, and leave to dry for about an hour.

Golden rules

- Let adhesive dry properly before finishing a wood floor.
- Ask your supplier for advice, and follow the manufacturer's instructions.
- Always test the finish on a hidden piece of floor or a scrap piece of flooring wood before you apply it to the whole floor.
- Work safely. Ventilate the room well and wear strong rubber gloves when applying the finish. Cloths soaked in sealant, particularly linseed-based finishes, and sawdust are both extremely flammable. Remove them from the house as quickly as possible, and dispose of them safely. If you are sanding, extinguish any gas pilot lights and do not light matches or any other type of flame.

PREPARING THE FLOOR FOR FINISHING

If you want to stain, paint or varnish prefinished wood you will have to remove the existing coating by sanding the floor. An unfinished wood floor with a rough surface will also have to be sanded until smooth. If boards are in good condition, sand with medium- and fine-grade sandpaper wrapped around a block of wood. Take care when using electric sanders (☛ page 117), as they can remove an unnecessary amount of wood and in inexperienced hands may gouge the floor. Finish the preparation by vacuuming well and then wiping the floor with a damp, clean cloth soaked in mineral spirits to remove dirt and dust.

If you are sealing newly laid planks that have been mechanically planed, simply remove any loose dirt particles by vacuuming and then wiping. Always ensure that any adhesive used has dried properly before applying a finish.

SEALING WOOD

Wood supplied without a varnish must be sealed to waterproof and otherwise protect the floor, and to enhance its color. There are various sealing products available, varying in strength and effect. If you're in any doubt about which finish to use on your floor, discuss it with your supplier.

Varnish

Polyurethane varnish is the simplest finish for amateurs to use, as it dries quickly (around 2 hours) and is less noxious to use than some other varnishes. Instructions for applying polyurethane varnish are given opposite, in the step-by-step guide to adding color. Polyurethane varnish is very versatile, as you can choose a full gloss, satin or matte finish, and it is also available in a range of colors. You can buy an acrylic version that dries even more quickly than alcohol-based polyurethane, but this coating is more difficult to maintain as it needs to be waxed more frequently (producing a beautiful luster).

Natural finishes

There are a variety of natural finishes available, including wax and oil (linseed, teak or "finishing oil"), most of which are more environmentally friendly than synthetic varnishes. They are also more straightforward to apply than varnish, though the process is usually more laborious if done by hand, and coats can take longer to dry.

Wax and oil both give wood a beautiful sheen. Wax is supplied in solid form, to be rubbed across the floor with a clean cloth, or as liquid that can be applied with an electric polisher (which may be rented). Apply two coats initially, leaving each coat to dry for 3 hours and polishing each coat. A single coat of wax should then be applied and polished twice yearly.

Similarly, oil can be applied by hand or using an electric floor polisher. Apply 2 coats initially, leaving each coat to dry for at least 4 hours. Polish each coat. A further application of oil is recommended at twice-yearly intervals, or more often if the finish appears to be wearing away.

TRADITIONAL PICKLING

Pickling is a traditional finish, used particularly on oak. It yields a bleached effect by highlighting the grain of the wood with a dense paste. If you do not wish to handle pickling paste (which is relatively toxic), create a similar effect by applying a coat of white emulsion paint instead, and then rubbing it off immediately with a clean, lint-free cloth. Seal with wax.

Step 1
Open up the wood grain by working along it (in the direction of the grain) with a wire brush. If the wood is also to be stained, follow the instructions below (*Adding color*), and leave to dry overnight.

Step 2
Apply a coat of pickling paste using a big pad of cotton wool covered in a clean linen cloth. Rub the paste across the grain to ensure that all the wood pores are filled.

Step 3
After 10 minutes remove the excess paste, again wiping across the grain. Allow the floor to dry for a few hours, until dry to the touch, then use the cloth-wrapped cotton-wool pad to polish, working across the grain. Apply a coat of clear varnish as protection.

ADDING COLOR

Wood floors are usually colored in two stages, first by staining for color and then varnishing for protection and luster. There are, however, an increasing number of stains that include varnish, for easy one-stage application. You can buy stain in a range of colors and effects (such as mahogany, pine or antique). Buy enough to cover the whole floor and repair any damage down the road, as mixing cans can result in a patchy covering. Before staining, the floor should be sanded, if necessary, and then vacuumed and wiped with a damp, clean cloth (using a lint-free cloth like cheesecloth) to remove all dirt. Stain baseboards and moldings before treating the floor itself.

Step 1
Fill a paint tray with wood stain, and apply it to the floor with a clean, lint-free cloth. Use long strokes and work in one direction (with the grain). Work the stain into the edges with a small paintbrush. Wait 10 minutes to allow the stain to penetrate the pores of the wood, then wipe off the surplus with a clean, lint-free cloth. Allow to dry overnight.

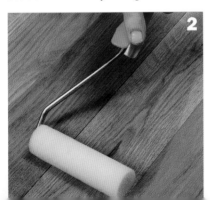

Step 3
Clean the floor with a vacuum cleaner, then wipe once again, and apply a second coat of polyurethane varnish, as in Step 2.

Step 2
When the stain has dried, vacuum and wipe with a clean, damp cloth to remove any dust. Then apply a coat of clear polyurethane varnish with a foam paint roller, using a ½ in. (1.25cm) paintbrush to work it into the edges and corners. Use long strokes and work with the grain. Allow 2 hours for the varnish to dry.

Other colored finishes

There are many colored varnishes available, which can be used to adjust or enhance the color of the floor and seal it at the same time. Prepare the floor as described in *Preparing the floor for finishing* (opposite), then apply two coats of colored varnish as shown in *Adding color*, omitting the wood stain. Allow about 2 hours for each coat to dry.

The floor may also be painted using one of the huge range of wood paints available. Prepare the floor as opposite, then apply a coat of wood primer to prevent the paint from sinking into the wood. Use a paint roller and paintbrush to apply the primer, and leave to dry for 2 hours. Then apply 2-3 coats of paint, allowing each one to dry overnight.

Renovating a wood floor

LEVEL OF DIFFICULTY

●○○○○

Renovating an existing floor does not require great skill, but sanding demands strength and endurance.

WARNING

SAWDUST IS EXTREMELY FLAMMABLE, AND HAS BEEN KNOWN TO CAUSE EXPLOSIVE HOUSE FIRES. REMOVE SAWDUST FROM THE HOUSE AS SOON AS POSSIBLE, AND DISPOSE OF IT ACCORDING TO LOCAL SAFETY REGULATIONS.

Toolbox

1 CHALK
2 SMALL METAL DETECTOR
3 CLAW HAMMER
4 CIRCULAR SAW/
   FINE-TOOTH HANDSAW
5 PRY BAR
6 COLD CHISEL
7 SCREWDRIVER
8 MALLET
9 PALETTE KNIFE
10 NAIL SET
11 FLOOR SCRAPER
12 DRUM SANDER
13 EDGE SANDER
14 LINT-FREE CLOTHS
   (LIKE CHEESECLOTH)

Materials

15 REPLACEMENT BOARDS
   AND OFFCUTS FOR GAPS
16 PLASTIC SHEETING
17 WOOD PRESERVATIVE
18 WOOD ADHESIVE
19 TALCUM POWDER
20 SAWDUST
21 WOOD FILLER
22 CHEMICAL STRIPPER
23 HOUSEHOLD DETERGENT
24 FINE-, MEDIUM- AND
   COARSE-GRADE
   SANDPAPER FOR SANDERS
25 MINERAL SPIRITS
26 SANDPAPER FOR
   HAND-SANDING

If you live in an older property, you may have an existing softwood or hardwood floor (ranging from basic pine floorboards to original parquet) that can be sanded and finished for stylish flooring at low cost. You may need to remove existing floor coverings to expose the boards below; if so, pull up a small section first to establish whether the floor is worth restoring and assess how much work will be involved in removing old nails and finishes. If the boards are veneered, check that the coat is thick enough for sanding.

Golden rules

- Work safely. Read the safety instructions before using electric sanders, and wear a face mask, safety glasses and ear protectors when sanding.
- Do not store sawdust in the house: keep it outside in a lidded metal container before disposing of it safely.
- If you are sanding, extinguish any gas pilot lights, and do not light matches or any other type of flame.

RESTORING WOOD BOARDS

Preparing the floor

Remove all floor coverings, then walk over the floor to locate loose or squeaking boards, holes to be filled and any sagging or rotten sections (rotten wood crumbles easily). Mark these areas with chalk. Establish the position of the joists by looking for nail-heads. You should avoid nailing, cutting or drilling between joists as this is where pipes and cables usually run (you could rent a small metal detector to identify the position of pipes). If you are going to sand, empty the room completely. Seal doors with plastic sheeting and open the windows.

USEFUL TIP

Check the position of pipes using a handheld metal detector. If you have to take up any boards, record the position of cables and pipes for future reference.

Step 1

If any boards are rotten or sagging, you will need to remove them by pulling out the nails from the joists with a claw hammer. If the nails are impossible to remove, cut the board out using a circular saw, taking care not to cut into the joists below. Then lever up the board and nails with a pry bar or cold chisel. If boards are tongued and grooved, strike off the tongues with a hammer and cold chisel before attempting to lift them.

Step 3

Sagging and squeaking are often caused by sagging joists. Insert a thin piece of wood coated with wood adhesive between the board and joist. Secure loose boards by screwing or nailing them firmly to the joists.

Step 2

Rotten boards must be replaced with new timber cut to size with a circular saw or fine-tooth handsaw. Treat the new boards with a coat of wood preservative and allow to dry. Then replace the boards, screwing or nailing them in place through the joists.

USEFUL TIP

If a board squeaks but you don't want to raise it, brush talcum powder into the joints from the surface of the floor.

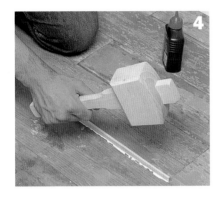

Step 4

Use a mallet to tap thin strips of wood coated with wood adhesive into narrow gaps. Alternatively, mix sawdust (available in bags from a lumber yard) with adhesive until you achieve a sticky paste, and insert this mixture into gaps with a palette knife. Wood filler can be used for small gaps and broken-away knots (a darker shade of filler usually looks more natural).

Step 6

Attach coarse-grade sandpaper to the drum sander. Move the sander the moment it touches the wood to avoid gouging the floor. Cross the room, working parallel to the grain. You may need to work on a diagonal if the boards are particularly rough, in which case you should remove the markings by sanding back along the diagonal, working in the opposite direction. If you are sanding herringbone parquet, follow the pattern and work in both directions.

Step 7

When you reach the far side of the room, work back across the floor, overlapping the previously sanded strip by about 2 in. (5cm). If the sandpaper tears or the dust bag fills up, unplug the machine and change the sandpaper or bag.

Step 9

Vacuum thoroughly. Then sand the whole floor again with medium-grade sandpaper, scraping behind obstacles like pipes with a palette knife. Repeat the process with fine-grade sandpaper, then vacuum again and wipe the floor with a clean, lint-free cloth soaked in mineral spirits. Fill any remaining holes and sand these areas by hand. Apply the first coat of finish (☞ pages 114–115) the day you finish sanding.

Step 5

Before sanding, push in any protruding nails with a hammer and nail set, or lever them up with a claw hammer. If the floor is painted, remove as much paint as you can with a chemical stripper and floor scraper to avoid clogging the sander. Mop off stripper with hot water and household detergent.

Step 8

When you have drum-sanded the floor, attach coarse-grade sandpaper to the edge sander, and work around the perimeter of the room.

Replacing all the floorboards

If the floorboards are in extremely bad condition, you may want to replace them all, using either ¾ in. (2cm) structural plywood or tongue-and-groove softwood floorboards (which may be used as a subfloor or left exposed). Softwood should be kept on site for 48 hours before installation to acclimatize. Remove baseboards and moldings before starting work.

If you are working on a ground floor, remove all the boards and inspect the joists for woodworm and rot, cutting away affected areas and treating the sound wood with wood preservative. Install waterproofing if required (☞ page 19) and make sure air vents are not blocked. If you are working on an upper story, remove and replace boards a row at a time to avoid having to balance on the joists. Simply face-nail the new boards or plywood panels to the joists, with boards or panels positioned so that they are perpendicular to the joists. Knock the tongues of the next row of softwood boards into the grooves of the laid row, or butt up the next plywood panel tightly against the first, and again nail to the joists. Continue until the floor is covered, using a circular saw or a fine-tooth handsaw to cut the material to fit. Ensure that each end of a board or panel is attached to a joist, and that the floor is rigid and secure.

Laminate

PROPERTIES AT A GLANCE

(*low, **medium, ***high)
- **LOW MAINTENANCE** **
- **HARD-WEARING** **
- **HEAT RETENTION** *
- **SOUND INSULATION** *
- **WATER RESISTANCE** *

The fastest growing sector of the floor-covering industry worldwide is laminated flooring. Laid as a floating floor, with boards that simply "click" together, this is the easiest wood floor for a non-professional to lay (and remove), requiring no nailing or gluing. Fierce competition between producers has also made laminate very affordable.

Laminated boards are made from high-density fiberboard (HDF), on which is attached one of an ever increasing range of simulated effects including almost every type of wood conceivable, as well as many hard-tile floors. Another clear layer, known as the "wear coat," protects the image. Underneath the HDF, there's often a thin sheet of melamine that acts as a moisture-protection layer. The grooves and tongues for the "click" system are machined around the edges of the boards.

Laminated flooring is not suitable for wet areas, especially bathrooms, as HDF is very sensitive to moisture and will quickly deteriorate. It can be laid in kitchens, but make sure you follow any advice aimed at preventing water from seeping into the joints or under the flooring. Plastic trays that fit under a dishwasher or washing machine can help, and are usually available from your flooring supplier. You must always put down waterproofing under any laminated floor, and your supplier will also recommend that you install a layer of foam underlayment, which adds bounce and increases the wear of the floor. Follow the supplier's recommendations to avoid invalidating the warranty.

Though reasonably hard-wearing (and often burn resistant), laminate is not as durable as wood, linoleum or good-quality

MARBLE

MARBLE

GRAPHITE

BRONZE

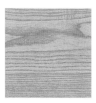

OAK

ANTIQUE WALNUT

PINE

MAPLE

Designing the floor

Laminate gives a room a bright feel, and can be more stylish than vinyl or carpet. Vinyl tiles may offer a greater range of effects and wider scope for creativity, but laminate provides a more realistic simulation of wood, and when it comes to hard tiles can compete with the best vinyl products. As with vinyl, the more expensive the flooring, the more impressive the simulation will be. You can buy boards with beveled edges to enhance the natural-wood effect, and the floors at the top end of the range feature convincing grain patterns. Also available are distressed boards, or boards with a stained or pickled (bleached) look. You can even buy planks of varying widths to increase the rustic feel, while some laminated images mimic the herringbone pattern of parquet flooring. If you would like to simulate a hard floor, choose from a range of ceramic, slate, stone or marble effects, all supplied with the easy-to-use "click" system.

To fully integrate the floor into its setting, your supplier can provide accessories to create a co-ordinated look, including matching transition moldings, thresholds, pipe covers, and baseboards to cover the expansion gap around the edges of the floor.

Top right: It's not only wood that can be simulated with laminate. A convincing impression of slate is achieved here with the use of "grout" lines.

Right: More expensive laminate boards feature grain patterns that enhance the realism of a wood simulation.

vinyl. Its main attraction lies in the amazing range of effects now available—at affordable prices. Laminate's ease of installation is also a strong selling point.

Maintenance

Gently sweep a laminated floor with a soft brush, as often as possible, to remove abrasive particles of dirt that can dull and damage the floor. You can wash laminated floors with a sponge mop, using diluted household detergent. Wring out the mop thoroughly before use, and make sure it is always clean to avoid scratching the floor with grit. Wipe up any spills immediately. Your supplier will offer a range of recommended cleaning products, and there are also some special enhancers available to increase the luster of the floor. These products are applied either by aerosol or with a mop, and are wiped off once dry.

Advantages
- Impressively realistic effects.
- Easy to install and maintain.
- Good range of options for all price brackets.
- No drafty gaps between boards.
- Particularly suitable for family rooms, hallways and children's bedrooms.

Disadvantages
- Not as warm as natural wood.
- Unsuitable for a damp environment.
- Not as durable as wood, linoleum or high-quality vinyl.
- Can be noisier than a natural wood floor.

Left: This laminate floor provides an excellent simulation of terra-cotta, and is cheaper and easier to install than the real thing. Bear in mind, however, that laminate simulations will be much less water-resistant and durable than stone.

Above: The brightness of laminate makes it particularly suitable for a contemporary interior.

Laying a laminated floor

LEVEL OF DIFFICULTY
●●○○○

A laminated floor, also called an engineered floor, is relatively easy to lay as no gluing or nailing is needed. Laminated boards are prefinished and do not need staining or sealing. Take care to avoid chipping laminate.

Toolbox
1 PAINT ROLLER (IF USING LIQUID DAMP-PROOF MEMBRANE)
2 UTILITY KNIFE
3 DUCT TAPE
4 CHALK LINE
5 TRY SQUARE
6 STRAIGHTEDGE
7 ½ IN. (1.25CM) SPACERS
8 TAPPING BLOCK
9 HAMMER
10 CLEAN CLOTHS
11 FINE-TOOTH HANDSAW/ PORTABLE CIRCULAR SAW
12 ELECTRIC DRILL WITH WOOD BIT
13 TAPPING BAR

Materials
14 LAMINATED BOARDS
15 POLYETHYLENE SHEET/LIQUID DAMP-PROOF MEMBRANE
16 FOAM UNDERLAYMENT
17 MATCHING WOOD FILLER
18 MATCHING MOLDINGS AND BASEBOARDS (IF DESIRED)

A floating laminated floor can be laid straight onto existing boards, and leveling with marine plywood is only necessary if these are in a bad condition. Similarly, you will only need to use leveling compound if a concrete subfloor is very uneven (☛ pages 18–19). Check if you need to trim doors (☛ page 21). If you can, remove vent grills, as well as moldings or baseboards (☛ page 20), which will be replaced later to hide the expansion gap. You should also make a floor plan to establish how many boards you need, and how wide the first and last rows should be. Adjust the plan if you have any very thin strips at the edges.

Laminate floors must always be underlaid with a damp-proof membrane and a cushioning foam underlayment. You can also buy underlayment composed of foam with a waterproof backing, which combines the two underlayments in one. Check with your supplier about the recommended underlayment and adhesive for your laminated boards.

Golden rules
- Prepare the site before starting (☛ pages 18–21).
- Buy all materials at the same time to guarantee consistency and availability.
- Ask your supplier for advice, and follow the manufacturer's instructions.
- Always check the site for moisture and underlay wood floors with waterproofing (☛ page 19). If moisture is present, consider laying a more water-resistant flooring.
- Work safely. Clamp boards firmly when sawing, wear a mask to avoid inhaling dust, and protect yourself from sharp laminate chips with safety glasses. Wear a mask, safety glasses, gloves and ear protection when using power tools.

INSTALLING LAMINATED BOARDS

Preparing the boards
Laminate swells and shrinks with changes in temperature and humidity so acclimatize the flooring by storing it on site for at least 48 hours before installation. Before you start, try a few test rows to check the effect of the staggered jointing, and saw off the tongues from the first row of boards. To establish a straight start line in Step 3, snap a chalk line along the longest, straightest wall, at a distance of the width of the first board, plus an expansion gap of ½ in. (1.25cm). If the wall is not straight, use a try square to establish a straight line. Extend this line along the floor with a straightedge, and use it as a guide when snapping the chalk line. Gaps caused by uneven walls can be filled later with wood filler or boards cut lengthwise, or covered by moldings.

Step 2
Lay the foam underlayment onto the polyethylene sheet, butting sheets together and joining them with duct tape. (You could use waterproofed foam underlayment instead, combining Steps 1 and 2.)

> **USEFUL TIP**
> Avoid overlapping sheets of underlayment, as the double thickness will show up when you lay the boards.

Step 1
Cover the subfloor with polyethylene sheet, overlapping joints by 2 in. (5cm), and sealing with duct tape. Leave at least 1 in. (2.5cm) lapping up the walls, to be trimmed back with a utility knife later or hidden by moldings or baseboards. Alternatively, paint on a coat of liquid damp-proof membrane with a paint roller, and leave to dry for a couple of hours. Plywood leveling is not usually needed. If it is, install plywood over the waterproofing (☛ page 18).

Step 3
Snap a chalk line marking the outer edge of what will be the first row of boards, as described above. Lay the first board against the chalk line, with its tongued edges toward the walls (sawing off the tongues themselves produces a neater fit). Insert ½ in. (1.25cm) spacers between the board and the walls to ensure a consistent expansion gap.

Step 4

Lower the second board of the first row to the floor, sliding the tongue at the end of the second board into the groove at the end of the first board, and clicking it into place. If necessary, use a tapping block and hammer to knock the board gently into position. Insert spacers between the second board and the wall, and push both boards up against the spacers. Then continue working along the chalk line, fitting spacers between the boards and the wall as you go.

Step 5

When you reach the end of the row, cut the last board to fit (☛ page 101), allowing for a ½ in. (1.25cm) expansion gap. Draw true lines with a try square and cut with a fine-tooth handsaw or portable circular saw. Saw from top to bottom to avoid splintering the top surface. Drill holes for pipes with an electric drill. Start the next row with the balance of the cut board to ensure board joints in adjacent rows are staggered for rigidity and effect. Stagger joints by at least 18 in. (46cm).

Step 6

Continue laying the floor, gently using the tapping block and hammer to help click tongues into grooves, and taking care not to strike chips off the laminate. (Wrapping the tapping block in a piece of soft cloth can help prevent chipping.) If you make a mistake and want to dismantle part of the floor, gently "unclick" the boards.

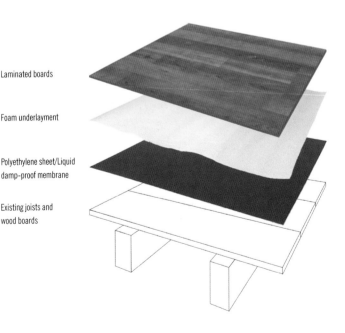

Step 7

Cut the boards in the final row lengthwise to fit (☛ page 101), allowing for a ½ in. (1.25cm) expansion gap. Slot the final boards into the previous row and use a tapping bar to click them into place. Also cut boards to fill any large gaps caused by uneven walls.

Step 8

Fill small gaps with matching filler. Wipe off any excess with a damp clean cloth, and leave to dry for about an hour.

Step 9

Trim back the polyethylene sheet at the edges, if necessary, and reinstall moldings (or baseboards if you have removed them) to cover the expansion gaps.

THE FLOORING LAYERS

Laying on a concrete subfloor

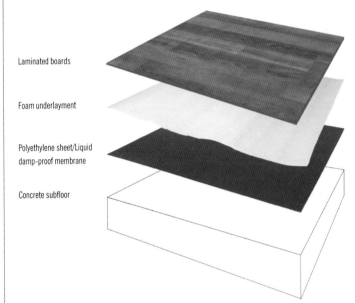

Laminated boards

Foam underlayment

Polyethylene sheet/Liquid damp-proof membrane

Concrete subfloor

Laying on a wood subfloor

Laminated boards

Foam underlayment

Polyethylene sheet/Liquid damp-proof membrane

Existing joists and wood boards

SOFT FLOORS

For comfort it's hard to beat a carpeted floor, especially during the winter. Carpet is probably the most widely available of floorings, so you won't be short of choice, whether you want plain or patterned, loop or cut pile, or any one of the spectrum of colors from white to black. Natural-fiber floorings, such as jute or sisal, have plenty of character and are environmentally friendly, too. Both carpet and natural-fiber coverings are tricky to lay, so you may need to employ a professional installer (the cost of installation is often priced into the product); alternatively, consider carpet tiles, which are easy to fit. However, carpet-laying is a skill well worth practicing: since carpets are ubiquitous you are bound to put your skills to use again in the future.

Installing soft floors

Soft floors (carpet and natural-fiber coverings) are among the most difficult to lay, since you must handle bulky rolls of covering and padding, and stretching the floor to a perfectly smooth finish is not easy. A simpler option is to use carpet tiles, which are small and light, and are installed as you would lay tiles like cork, but unfortunately carpet tiles for domestic use tend to be low quality and limited in range. Most soft floors involve the installation of padding, tackless strips (also called tack strips) and transition moldings, and the use of some special tools.

KNEE KICKER

STAIR TOOLS

How suitable is the subfloor?

Broadloom carpet (supplied as a roll) is always underlaid with padding, and padding is often installed under natural-fiber floors, too. Padding will absorb a certain amount of unevenness, so a perfectly smooth subfloor is not as vital as with some other flooring. If the subfloor is in poor condition, however, you will still need to apply leveling compound or an extra layer of marine plywood (☞ pages 18–19). If you are not using padding at all, you should always level the floor before installation.

Certain floors require the use of carpet or natural-fiber adhesive, spread in a thin layer, which enables you to pull up laid material in order to reposition it. In this case, it is very important to ensure the subfloor is clean, since dust may prevent the thin layer of adhesive from sticking properly.

Acclimatizing the flooring

Natural-fiber soft floor coverings will shrink or swell in response to changes in ambient temperature and humidity, and for that reason should be kept on site, in normal living conditions, for at least 48 hours before cutting or fitting. Carpet does not need to be conditioned in this way.

CARPET SHEARS

Choosing padding

Padding is installed under carpet and natural-fiber flooring to give the floor extra cushioning and increase the life of the covering. Padding is usually made from polyurethane foam, bonded polyurethane, rubber or fiber, although lightweight alternatives are being developed. Ask your supplier to recommend a padding that suits both the flooring and the site, and buy the best you can afford. A thick, soft padding is normally chosen for comfortable areas of low traffic, such as bedrooms, with thinner padding used for more hard-wearing areas, such as stairs. Remember that padding used for carpet is not the same as that laid under natural-fiber floors.

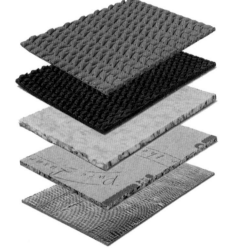

TECHNIQUES FOR SOFT FLOORS

CARPET CUTTER

Cutting soft flooring

Carpet and natural-fiber flooring can be cut easily with a sharp utility knife (and plenty of spare blades), or carpet shears, and a straightedge. Use carpet shears for loop-pile carpet. If you wish, you can purchase special cutting tools such as an edge trimmer, but a utility knife works just as well. Cut tackless strips with metal snips or a hacksaw.

If you are flooring a room much narrower than the width of your covering, cut the material roughly to size in a larger area before moving it to the site. Leave at least a 2 in. (5cm) excess all around; this will be trimmed and tucked behind the tackless strips, and may also be hidden by moldings.

Most carpets are cut from the back. You can mark a cutting line on the backing using felt-tip pen. Loop-pile carpets, however, are cut from the top along a line opened between the loops with a screwdriver. Natural-fiber coverings can also be cut from the top.

CARPET TRIMMER

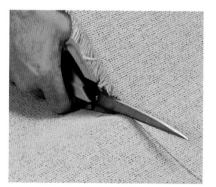

CUTTING WITH CARPET SHEARS

CUTTING WITH A UTILITY KNIFE

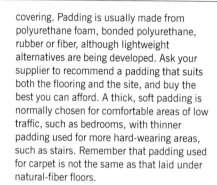

Seaming

If you need to join two or more sections to cover a large site or to fit into recesses, plan the layout to ensure that seams are in low traffic areas and as invisible as possible. The cut of the pile may make the surface of the carpet look different from different angles, so ensure that the pile on all pieces runs in the same direction, and that any patterns or borders are aligned.

Natural-fiber coverings are seamed by simply cutting and gluing them to the floor, but you will need to use a seaming iron to join pieces of carpet.

If seaming carpet, place a strip of hot-glue seaming tape under the edges. Then slowly move a heated seaming iron under the carpet to melt the adhesive.

As you move forward, the two edges will fall back down onto the adhesive. Use weights to ensure that the carpet edges adhere firmly to the tape.

Stretching

Stretch carpet and natural-fiber flooring to ensure a perfect fit. Power stretchers are not recommended for use by amateurs, as they are extremely difficult to handle and may easily rip the carpet—many professional fitters prefer not to use them. Instead, work slowly and safely across the room using a knee kicker. Adjust the teeth of the knee kicker until its head grips the carpet backing without breaking through it. Then knock firmly with your leg (just above the knee) on the padded knee piece, pushing the carpet toward the wall and easing out any slackness.

Securing the edges

Carpets and natural-fiber coverings laid with padding are held in place at the edges of the room by tackless strips (also called tack strips). These are lengths of wood (sometimes metal), usually about 4ft. (1.2m) long, with pins that protrude at an angle. ("Blind" tackless strips, used for natural-fiber flooring, do not have pins.)

Ask your supplier to recommended a tackless strip for your subfloor. Standard strips for wood subfloors are nailed down. If you are laying tackless strips on concrete, drill through the strip and into the concrete, using a masonry bit, and secure with masonry nails. (Check first that the concrete will hold the nails.) Also available are tackless strips designed for floors, such as stone, that are too hard to take nails. These are glued with special adhesive available from your supplier.

Tackless strips are installed before the padding is laid. They should always be positioned with the pins pointing toward the wall. Some types of tackless strip do not have pins, but all have the manufacturer's name printed on the wood, and this should face toward you, so that you can read it.

Step 1
Position the tackless strip parallel to the wall, with a gap between strip and wall equal to just less than the thickness of the flooring (not including padding). Use a piece of wood as a spacer. The pins should point toward the wall, and the manufacturer's name should face you. Secure the strip to the subfloor.

Step 2
To attach the flooring, stretch it toward the tackless strip with a knee kicker and use a cold chisel to press it down onto the pins. Smooth with your hand, too. Then tuck the edge of the flooring neatly between the tackless strip and the wall with a stair tool.

TACKLESS STRIP

Flooring transitions

Where a soft covering meets another floor, typically in a doorway, a transition molding such as a carpet bar, threshold or Z-bar binding strip will be required. Transition moldings for soft floors are usually nailed or screwed to the subfloor at the same time as the tackless strips.

Carpet bars are used to join floorings of equal height, or when the covering is higher than the adjacent floor. They grip the flooring between a series of pins and a fold-over flange. Fix the carpet bar to the subfloor before the covering is fitted. When the covering is in place, trim the doorway edge to ⅛–¼ in. (3–6mm) short of the flange crease. Then stretch the covering using a knee kicker so that it fits into the bar, up to the beginning of the crease. Press the flooring onto the pins, and then fold over the flange, knocking it into place with a hammer and some scrap wood.

If a covering is at a lower level than the adjacent floor, attach a tackless strip to the subfloor, as described above, and press the flooring onto the pins as if the higher flooring were a wall. If two carpets of different thickness or appearance meet in a doorway, screw down a wood threshold between the two, installing a tackless strip next to the threshold to secure the carpet. If two carpets are of equal thickness and you prefer them to meet without a bar, join the floors using hot-glue seaming tape and a seaming iron. Alternatively, you can install a Z-bar binding strip, nailed under a length of tackless strip. Wrap the flooring over the Z-bar to hide the strip.

CARPET BAR

Z-BAR BINDING STRIP

METAL STRIP

WOOD THRESHOLD

Carpet

PROPERTIES AT A GLANCE
(*low, **medium, ***high)
- HEAT RETENTION ***
- SOUND INSULATION ***
- HARD-WEARING **
- LOW MAINTENANCE *
- WATER RESISTANCE *

Wall-to-wall carpet brings warmth and comfort to a home, making it a place for kicking off shoes and relaxing; no wonder it's so popular in living rooms, dens and bedrooms. Choosing a carpet, however, is not straightforward: the range of color, pattern, texture, quality and price is enormous. This means that you will always be able to find a carpet to suit your needs and budget—you just need time to consider all the options. Manufacturers grade carpets as to their ability to withstand wear: heavy domestic wear (living and family rooms, hallways, stairs and landings); general domestic (bedrooms) and light domestic (spare rooms). You should also consider the fiber mix, which may be 100 percent wool, 100 percent synthetic or a mixture of the two in varying proportions. It's still difficult to beat wool for comfort, wear and flame resistance, but wool tends also to be the most expensive. The main disadvantage of synthetic fibers is their low resistance to flame, and they also never look quite as buoyant as wool. Many carpets are an 80 percent wool/20 percent nylon mix. In high-moisture areas like bathrooms, a high synthetic mix can allow the carpet to dry quickly and prevent mildew from forming. There's great variety in the life of carpets: a good-quality, heavy-weight frieze (or hard twist) carpet in 80 percent wool/20 percent nylon will last up to 15 years, while a cheap lightweight synthetic carpet may flatten out in only a year or two.

Today the vast majority of domestic carpets are what's known as "tufted." During the manufacturing process, rows of

---

PATTERNED WOVEN

TWIST TUFTED

HIGHER-GRADE TWIST

VELVET

PATTERNED WOVEN

TWIST TUFTED

HIGHER-GRADE TWIST

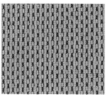

FLATWEAVE

Designing the floor

The nature of the pile will affect your choice of carpet. The loops of yarn may be long or short, thick or thin, straight or twisted, cut or uncut. Cut pile is smooth and gives a formal effect, but tends to show footprints (although it doesn't necessarily wear less well than loop pile). The loops of loop pile are left uncut: these carpets are more textured and casual in appearance, and resist pressure marks. Thick-cut pile softens a room, but may lose its "bounce" in doorways and high-traffic areas. A very long pile, like shag, is comfortable but hard to keep clean. Here are some of the most common types of carpet:

Saxony

Probably the most popular style of tufted carpet in North America is cut-pile Saxony, usually sold in solid colors with a long pile. It is best in the heavier weights, when the tufts are condensed to produce a dense, durable surface. Unfortunately, this style tends to show footmarks and vacuum cleaner lines. Available in a wide range of pile weights, the heavier ones are suitable for living rooms, halls, stairs and landings, with lighter weights ideal for bedrooms.

Berber

Berber style is a loop pile, traditionally in pale natural shades but now sold in many different colors. Available in a range of fibers, Berber can be used in most areas of the home.

Cut and loop

This combines the robustness of a loop face with the formal look of a cut pile. The combination gives a pleasing, textured effect. Cut and loop is inexpensive, and can be used in most places, although it will flatten in high-traffic areas like hallways, stairs and landings.

Left: There is huge variety in the appearance and performance of different styles of carpet, so discuss all your requirements with your supplier before making a purchase.

Right: By far the most popular type of carpet in North America today, Saxony offers comfort and durability, especially in the heavier weights.

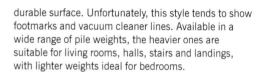

needles feed the yarn through a polypropylene backing sheet in a continuous series of loops. These loops form the pile, and may be cut, left looped, or cut and looped, each version dictating the look, feel and wear of the carpet. The weight and height of the yarn loops also determine the appearance of the pile.

Carpets were originally hand-woven, on a loom, and it is still possible to buy woven-wool carpets. Axminster and Wilton are the best-known styles. They are durable, expensive and often highly patterned, and these days are mostly used in a commercial context. Woven carpets are more expensive than tufted because the yarn is costly and the technique of manufacture time-consuming, but they also have a longer life than the cheaper grades of tufted. Good-quality tufted and woven carpets of a similar pile weight will, however, have a comparable life. Carpets with a tightly woven backing last

Advantages
- Warm and comfortable underfoot.
- Available in a wide variety of colors, patterns and textures.
- Prices range from budget to expensive.
- Good sound insulation.
- Particularly suitable for bedrooms and upstairs rooms in general, hallways, stairs, and family and living rooms.

Disadvantages
- Easily marked by dirt and spills, and difficult to clean.
- Can harbor dust that may exacerbate allergies and asthma (sometimes avoided in children's rooms for this reason).
- Not suitable for kitchens, and doesn't cope well with moisture unless highly synthetic.

Above: Supplied in every shade imaginable, carpet is the easiest type of flooring to match exactly to your walls and furnishings.

Below: An 80 percent wool/20 percent nylon blend produces a carpet that combines durability with the comfort, texture and visual appeal of wool.

Above: Carpet with twisted pile offers resistance to footmarks and other pressure marks.

longer than those with a looser weave. Woven carpets are supplied with or without pile: those without pile are known as "flatweave."

The cheapest carpets are "non-woven." These are constructed by gluing synthetic fibers to a backing, and are often produced in the form of carpet tiles. Although much less durable than other forms of carpet, non-woven carpet tiles can be useful for small areas or where access to under-floor services is needed. Worn tiles are easy to replace without requiring the removal of the entire floor.

One exciting development has been the introduction of carpet fibers made from recycled garbage such as soft drinks containers. Carpets produced in this way tend to be coarse and best suited to commercial and industrial uses, but no doubt the technique will be refined in the future to create products that are both attractive and environmentally friendly.

Maintenance

Vacuum carpets at least once a week. To remove odor and break down ground-in dirt, spray carpet-cleaning powder over the

Left: Wall-to-wall carpet is the cosiest of all flooring and can also bring a sense of style and luxury to a family home.

Velvet
A cut pile, velvet is soft and smooth, and looks very attractive. It is also fairly durable, but keep in mind that plain cut-pile carpets have a tendency to show up footmarks and vacuum cleaner lines.

Frieze
This cut-pile style (also known as hard twist) has tufts with a tight twist that reduces the effect of footmarks, while producing a smooth carpet without the drawbacks of velvet. This style is suitable for most areas of the home, and the heavier weights fare well in areas of high traffic. At the heaviest end of the range there are various "crush resistor" options.

Low-level loop
Usually made of nylon fiber, low-level loop is available in a wide color choice, including a "tweed" effect that combines a number of different colors in the yarn. It is very durable and suitable for family rooms and children's bedrooms, but doesn't cope well with water.

Above: Not all woven carpets feature the lurid patterning associated with hotels. These subtle diamond motifs produce a light and lively effect, without being overbearing.

Opposite: Striped carpeting will grab the attention, but bear in mind that the more patterned the carpet, the plainer the walls should be.

floor, and then vacuum it up. Once the carpet begins to lose its color, or after a party, you may want to give it a proper cleaning. You can make use of a professional carpet-cleaning service; otherwise, a range of wet or dry detergents are available, which are applied by a cleaning machine and then vacuumed up, immediately or later. Steam carpet cleaners are the most readily available machines (those that work by brushing into the carpet may damage some piles, particularly deeper) and can be rented, usually from a hardware or grocery store. Before you start, vacuum the carpet well to remove all loose dirt. Clear away as

much furniture as you can and use plastic film or bubble wrap to protect the legs of the pieces that you can't move. When cleaning, be careful not to use too much water or you may damage the carpet backing. For faster drying, ventilate the room and leave it empty for about two hours or until the carpet is absolutely dry.

Left: For a totally original floor, ask your installer to customize a carpet to your design specifications. Here, colored insets form a "rug" in a fitted carpet.

Right: A pure-wool, all-white carpet with embossed patterning brings an atmosphere of luxury to a room.

Left: A delicate floral pattern can recreate the atmosphere of times past, and lend elegance to a bedroom.

Laying a carpeted floor

Carpet is available as both broadloom (supplied as a roll) and tiles, and the two varieties are installed differently. Broadloom is bulky and much more difficult to handle than tiles. It is also underlaid with thick padding, which means that you will not need to level the subfloor unless it is very uneven. Tiles, however, are not underlaid with padding, so you should level a concrete floor with leveling compound and cover wood floorboards with ¼ in. (6mm) marine plywood treated with diluted PVA adhesive (☞ pages 18–19). Tiles are laid with special carpet adhesive spread in a thin layer, so ensure that the subfloor is clean, otherwise dust may render the adhesive ineffective. This adhesive will allow you to peel up a tile and lay another in its place should the flooring become damaged or excessively worn.

Test whether you need to trim doors (☞ page 21) by checking their clearance over a scrap piece of carpet and a transition molding. Calculate how much carpet you need by drawing a plan of the area, and buy wider widths to avoid seaming. If you are laying tiles, make a floor plan to calculate how many you need, and map out any design to ensure an accurate layout (☞ pages 12–15).

Golden rules

- **Prepare the site before starting (☞ pages 18–21).**
- **Measure the room carefully to make the best use of carpet widths, and avoid seaming if possible.**
- **Ask your supplier for advice when buying padding, tackless strips (also called tack strips) and transition moldings. Always follow the manufacturer's instructions.**
- **Work safely. Ventilate the room well when using adhesive. Take care when exerting pressure on your utility knife and when handling tackless strips.**

LEVEL OF DIFFICULTY
●●●●●

Broadloom carpet is bulky and difficult to maneuver. You will need to install padding, tackless strips and transition moldings, and you may also need to seam pieces of carpet together.

Toolbox

1 HAMMER
2 DRILL WITH MASONRY BIT (FOR A CONCRETE SUBFLOOR)
3 METAL SNIPS
4 UTILITY KNIFE AND EXTRA BLADES/CARPET SHEARS
5 STRAIGHTEDGE
6 DUCT TAPE
7 STAPLE GUN (FOR A WOOD SUBFLOOR)
8 SCREWDRIVER (FOR LOOP-PILE CARPET)
9 SEAMING IRON
10 WEIGHTS (SUCH AS A TOOLBOX)
11 KNEE KICKER
12 COLD CHISEL
13 STAIR TOOL
14 VACUUM CLEANER/BROOM

Materials

15 BROADLOOM CARPET
16 TACKLESS STRIPS
17 CARPET BAR/ THRESHOLD/Z-BAR BINDING STRIP
18 CARPET PADDING
19 PADDING ADHESIVE (FOR A CONCRETE SUBFLOOR)
20 HOT-GLUE SEAMING TAPE

INSTALLING BROADLOOM CARPET

Preparing the carpet

Plan where seams (if required) will fall before you start the installation, avoiding areas of high traffic. If the carpet is much bigger than the floor you are laying, cut it roughly to size in a larger area before transporting it to the site for installation. Leave 2 in. (5cm) at each edge for trimming. You can use a handheld metal detector to check for pipes before nailing tackless strips into the subfloor.

CARPET BARS

Step 1
Nail down the appropriate tackless strips for your floor (☞ page 125) along the edges of the room. Use a hammer on wood subfloors and a drill with a masonry bit on concrete. Install the strips at a distance from the wall of just less than the thickness of the carpet, with their pins pointing up and toward the wall. Use metal snips to cut them to fit between obstacles such as pipes and vents.

Step 2
Nail or screw down a carpet bar, threshold, Z-bar binding strip or tackless strip in the doorway, depending on your chosen method of carpet transition (☞ page 125).

Step 3
Unroll the padding to cover the floor, with any slippery side face up. Cut the padding to size using a straightedge and a utility knife or carpet shears, butting it up against the tackless strips. Do not overlap pieces of padding. Seal any seams with duct tape. Secure the padding with a staple gun, with staples every inch (2.5cm) around the edges and at 6 in. (15cm) intervals across the rest of the room. If your subfloor is concrete, use padding adhesive, thinly applied.

Step 4
Starting from the longest, straightest wall, unroll the carpet until you reach the opposite side of the room. The slant of the pile should face the most used doorway (to find pile direction, brush your palm across the carpet's surface or look for an arrow on its underside). Position the carpet and make slits at the corners of the room to allow the carpet to lie flat.

Step 5
Trim the edges to fit with a utility knife, cutting from the underside of the carpet. (If you are laying loop-pile carpet, cut from the top side of the carpet to avoid damaging the loops. Run a screwdriver through the loops along the straightedge to open a cutting path, and cut with carpet shears.) Cut slits to accommodate pipes and other obstacles. Then measure and cut any smaller pieces of carpet necessary to cover the floor, including inside closets.

USEFUL TIP
Lay a piece of scrap wood under the cutting area to avoid damaging carpet or padding.

Step 6
Make any seams required before stretching the carpet. Remember that the pile must run in the same direction over all pieces of carpet, and any pattern or border must also be aligned. When creating a seam, overlap the two pieces by about 3 in. (7.5cm), and cut through both thicknesses at the same time, using a utility knife (or shears if you are cutting loop-pile carpet), to create a perfect fit. Use a long straightedge to keep the seam straight. If there are pattern lines, use these as a cutting guide.

Step 7
Cut a strip of hot-glue seaming tape to fit, and position it under the seam. Hold a heated seaming iron on top of the seaming tape, under the two pieces of carpet, and move it slowly along the tape, letting the adhesive melt before you move forward. As you proceed, push the two pieces of carpet onto the melted adhesive, and place weights (such as a toolbox or books) over the seam (☛ page 125). Leave the adhesive to dry for at least an hour.

THE FLOORING LAYERS

Laying on a concrete subfloor

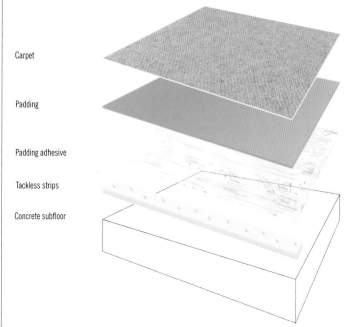

Carpet

Padding

Padding adhesive

Tackless strips

Concrete subfloor

Laying on a wood subfloor

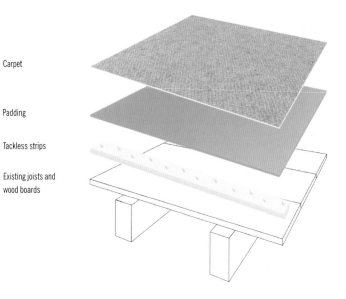

Carpet

Padding

Tackless strips

Existing joists and wood boards

Step 8

In one corner, start attaching the carpet to the tackless strips. Push the carpet toward the wall with a knee kicker. Then use the flat blade of a cold chisel to push the carpet onto the tackless strip, and tuck in the carpet edge between the wall and tackless strip with a stair tool. Continue moving along the first wall until you have secured about 2 ft. (0.6m) of carpet.

Step 9

Use the knee kicker to stretch the carpet from the secured area to the opposite wall, pushing the carpet right up to the tackless strip.

Step 10

Trim off any excess, if necessary, with your utility knife. Press the carpet onto the tackless strips with your hand and a cold chisel, and then use the stair tool to tuck the carpet between the tackless strip and wall. Return to the starting wall and move a little way down the room to repeat the process. When you have secured the whole carpet, check for any remaining looseness and, if necessary, stretch, trim and secure again. Fit the carpet at the doorway into your chosen transition bar page 125). Finally, sweep and vacuum the floor to remove trimmings.

LEVEL OF DIFFICULTY

●○○○○

Carpet tiles are light, and easy to cut and fit into awkward corners.

Toolbox

1 CHALK LINE
2 HAMMER
3 UTILITY KNIFE AND EXTRA BLADES
4 STRAIGHTEDGE/RULER
5 PAINT ROLLER
6 LINOLEUM ROLLER
7 VACUUM CLEANER/BROOM

Materials

8 CARPET TILES
9 CARPET BAR/ THRESHOLD/Z-BAR BINDING STRIP
10 KRAFT PAPER/CARD
11 CARPET ADHESIVE

INSTALLING CARPET TILES

Preparing the tiles

Mark two chalk lines at right angles across the center of the room, to act as guides in laying out the floor, and adjust them according to the quarter method (page 14). If you would like a border of contrasting tiles, start by laying this out first (page 15). Note that tiles are marked on the back with arrows to show the direction of the pile (which can also be identified by brushing your hand along the tile surface). Carpet tiles tend to look best with each tile twisted through 90 degrees from the position of the last tile, but you can also lay tiles with all arrows pointing in the same direction (to mimic the look of broadloom carpet). Do not mix the methods. Laying tiles dry first will enable you to check the overall effect.

Step 1

Nail or screw down a carpet bar, threshold or Z-bar binding strip in the doorway, depending on your chosen method of carpet transition (page 125).

Step 2

Lay the tiles without adhesive along the chalk lines, fitting them closely together. Then fill in the spaces between the chalk lines, working from the center of the room out, until the entire floor, except the edges, is laid out dry. As you work, check the arrows on the backs of the tiles. Twist each tile through 90 degrees from the position of the last one or lay all tiles with the pile running in the same direction. Check the overall effect before fixing.

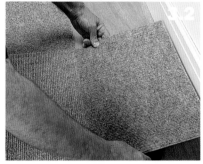

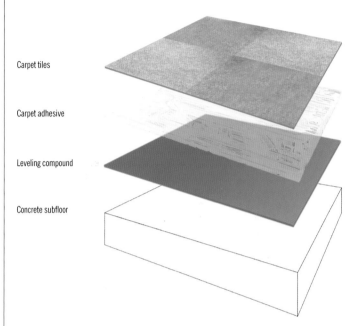

THE FLOORING LAYERS

Laying on a concrete subfloor

Carpet tiles

Carpet adhesive

Leveling compound

Concrete subfloor

Step 5
Once the entire floor is laid out dry, and you are happy with the overall effect, lift a section of about 10 tiles in the corner furthest from the exit. Pour a little adhesive onto the floor, and spread with a paint roller until the exposed section is thinly covered.

Step 3
Slip the edge tile under the last whole tile to cut it to fit, butting it up against the wall. Cut from the underside with a utility knife and extra blades. A straightedge or ruler will help you draw straight lines. The tiles' synthetic backing will ensure that edges do not fray.

Step 4
Cut tiles to fit around corners, pipes and vents, remembering to cut from the underside of the tile. You may find it helpful to use a Kraft paper or card template (pages 92–93) for complicated areas.

Step 6
Working toward the exit, start to lay the tiles onto the adhesive. Butt the tiles up tightly, and press down firmly as you lay each one. As you work, use the arrows on the back of the tiles to check pile direction and lay the tiles according to your chosen layout method. Then lift another section of tiles, and continue as above until the floor is laid.

Step 7
Use a linoleum roller to press the tiles firmly into the adhesive and remove any air bubbles. Work the roller in all directions, (starting at the center), and press down awkward corners with your fingers.

Step 8
Fit the carpet at the doorway into your chosen transition bar (page 125). Leave the adhesive to dry overnight, then sweep and vacuum the room to remove trimmings.

Laying on a wood subfloor

Carpet tiles

Carpet adhesive

¼ in. (6mm) marine plywood treated with diluted PVA adhesive

Existing joists and wood boards

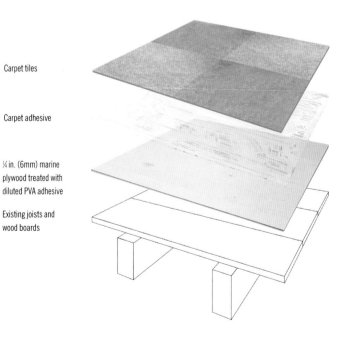

Natural fiber

PROPERTIES AT A GLANCE
(*low, **medium, ***high)
• HEAT RETENTION **
• SOUND INSULATION **
• HARD-WEARING *
• LOW MAINTENANCE *
• WATER RESISTANCE *

Natural-fiber floorings go in and out of fashion, but from an environmental point of view they are always a good choice. Most of these products are created in Third World countries, using traditional looms, and materials are largely from sustainable sources with replanting programs (though you should check with your supplier if sustainability concerns you). Natural-fiber floorings are biodegradable and much more "green" than carpet, and their sale can enable communities to gain currency from their local resources.

Natural-fiber floors include sisal, seagrass, jute and coir, all woven on a loom and coated with a latex backing to prevent fraying when cut to size. You can lay these floorings with or without padding: using padding adds to the price but makes the floor more comfortable and extends its life.

Natural-fiber flooring enjoys some of the benefits of carpet, being relatively soft and warm, and in addition offers a pleasantly natural appearance. These types of flooring also compare most favorably with carpet for cost. If laid with padding and kept clean, natural-fiber flooring is almost as durable as carpet—but, like carpet, it marks easily, and stains are very hard to remove. The tendency of natural-fiber flooring to stain and trap food particles makes it unsuitable for use in kitchens, and it can also be badly damaged by water, so is not ideal for use in bathrooms either. Some products may be too

SISAL

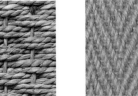

SEAGRASS

DYED SISAL

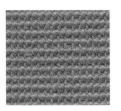

BAMBOO STRIP RUG

COIR

JUTE

DYED SISAL

WOVEN PAPER

Designing the floor

Natural-fiber flooring is available in many colors, textures and patterns—so explore what is available in your area. These floors are usually chosen for their natural appeal, and shades of beige, brown and green, bleached or unbleached, are the most popular, but you can also buy colors such as rust or dark blue, with new shades coming out all the time. Designs available include basketweave, herringbone and bouclé, some of which are woven with contrasting colors. The width of the twisted fibers varies from brand to brand, and weaves may be open or closed. Different products have different characteristics, so make sure you pick a flooring that is suitable for your site.

Sisal

Often sold in earth tones, sisal also comes in a range of other colors. The fiber was initially developed for rope-making, so is very strong and produces a relatively durable floorcovering. Sisal is most often woven in a simple loop design, but a bird's eye pattern is also frequently available, and it is also often supplied in interwoven colored stripes. This is the most expensive natural flooring, but also one of the most popular, thanks to its prominent yet relatively smooth texture, the tightness of the weave and the wide range of designs and colors available.

Opposite: Jute is an extraordinarily fine natural fiber with softness and a silky luster. It is ideal for bedrooms and low-traffic living areas.

Left: Although usually known for its natural appeal, sisal is also supplied in a range of dyed shades to suit your decoration scheme.

slippery or coarse for use on stairs (but if used, ensure the weave runs across the tread to give more grip).

Maintenance

As mentioned, stains are very hard to remove from natural-fiber flooring, and most of these products mark easily, so deal with spills immediately. As a protective measure, spray the product with stain-inhibitor before installation or buy flooring that has been pretreated by the manufacturer (note that seagrass has a natural resistance to stains). Vacuum or sweep the floor at least once a week. Avoid using both water and steam on soft natural flooring, as moisture will cause shrinking or buckling (depending on the floor), and even rotting.

Advantages
- Uses materials from sustainable sources.
- Many of the benefits of carpet at a cheaper price.
- Some coverings are soft enough for bedrooms, others are durable enough for hallways and high-traffic rooms.

Disadvantages
- Difficult to clean.
- Can harbor dust that may exacerbate allergies and asthma (sometimes avoided in children's rooms for this reason).
- Unsuitable for kitchens, bathrooms and other damp areas. May be too slippery for stairs.

Seagrass

Seagrass is impermeable to water, meaning that it is stain resistant and also that it cannot be dyed. It is therefore sold only in natural tones (sometimes with dyed fibers from other plants woven in for color). Seagrass is the smoothest of these floorings (perhaps too smooth to be safe on stairs), and comes in various designs such as herringbone and basketweave. Since it is stain resistant and fairly durable, seagrass can be used in more hard-working environments than other natural fibers.

Jute

Jute was originally used as sackcloth, and as backing for traditional carpets, but has now become a floorcovering in its own right. It has a soft surface and can be woven into a number of designs. Usually stone colored, jute is also dyed blue, green, red and other colors. Softer and less durable than other natural-fiber floorings, jute is used mostly for bedroom carpets.

Coir

Produced from the husks of coconuts, coir floorcovering comes in a variety of designs—bouclé, herringbone and basketweave are the most popular. It is usually a dark brown shade, although bleached coir, a pale-yellow color, has been introduced in recent years. Coir is too rough for bedrooms and its loose weave can be dangerous on stairs.

Above: The rougher texture of coir may make it unsuitable for some living environments, such as bedrooms.

Laying a natural-fiber floor

A natural-fiber floor can be laid with or without padding. Buy padding and adhesive made specially for natural-fiber floors, not carpet padding or carpet adhesive. Your supplier will be able to recommend suitable products. If you are laying a natural-fiber floor without padding, ensure that the subfloor is level, smoothing an uneven concrete floor with leveling compound and covering wood floorboards with ¼ in. (6mm) marine plywood treated with diluted PVA adhesive (☛ pages 18–19 for detailed instructions for preparing the site). If you are installing padding, you do not need to level the subfloor unless it is very uneven. In both cases, ensure that the subfloor is clean, as otherwise dust may prevent the adhesive, which is spread in a thin layer, from working properly.

Check whether you need to trim existing doors (☛ page 21) by testing their clearance over a scrap piece of flooring and a threshold molding. Calculate how much floor covering you need by drawing a plan of the area (☛ page 14).

Golden rules
- **Prepare the site before starting** (☛ pages 18–21).
- **Measure the room carefully to make the best use of widths of flooring, and avoid seaming if possible.**
- **Ask your supplier for advice when buying adhesive, padding and tackless strips, and always follow the manufacturers' instructions.**
- **Take care not to get adhesive onto the flooring: stains are almost impossible to remove from natural-fiber products.**
- **Work safely. Ventilate the room well and wear strong rubber gloves when working with adhesive.**

LEVEL OF DIFFICULTY
●●●●○
Like carpet, natural-fiber floorings are bulky and difficult to maneuver. It is not easy to achieve a perfectly smooth finish.

Toolbox
1 HAMMER
2 UTILITY KNIFE AND EXTRA BLADES
3 STRAIGHTEDGE
4 PAINTER'S TAPE
5 ⅛ IN. (3MM) NOTCHED TROWEL/PAINT ROLLER
6 KNEE KICKER
7 LINOLEUM ROLLER
8 STAIR TOOL

Materials
9 NATURAL-FIBER FLOORING
10 CARPET BAR/ THRESHOLD/Z-BAR BINDING STRIP
11 ADHESIVE (FOR NATURAL-FIBER FLOORING)

INSTALLING A NATURAL-FIBER FLOOR WITHOUT PADDING

Preparing the roll

To avoid shrinkage after the floor is laid, acclimatize natural-fiber flooring to the surroundings by keeping it on site for at least 48 hours before installation. If seams are required, plan where they will fall to avoid areas of high traffic. If the covering is much bigger than the floor area, cut it roughly to size in a larger area before transporting it to the site for installation. Leave about 2 in. (5cm) at the edges for trimming.

Step 1
Nail or screw a carpet bar, threshold or Z-bar binding strip to the subfloor in the doorway, depending on your chosen method of flooring transition (☛ page 125). Any pins should be pointing up and away from the flooring.

Step 2
First lay out the flooring dry. Starting from your longest, straightest wall, roll out the flooring to cover the subfloor. Use a sharp utility knife and a straightedge to trim the edges to fit, cutting into recesses and doorways, and around pipes. Change blades frequently. Make small slits in each of the corners to allow the flooring to lie flat (avoid cutting into the floor area).

Step 3
If you need to join sections of flooring, leave them overlapping by about 3 in. (7.5cm), secured with painter's tape, until all the other cutting and laying has been done and the covering fits perfectly at the edges. Then cut through both pieces simultaneously, using the utility knife and straightedge, to create edges that match exactly. (Do not try to butt up the pieces selvage to selvage as they will not be straight enough.)

THE FLOORING LAYERS

Laying on a concrete subfloor

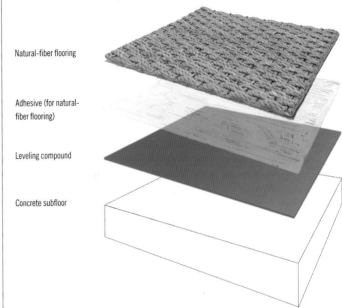

Step 4
Roll back the flooring at the end of the room furthest from the exit, until half the subfloor is exposed. Pour adhesive onto the floor and spread with a notched trowel or paint roller until the exposed section is thinly covered.

Step 6
When the entire floor is laid, use the knee kicker to remove any remaining looseness. Use a linoleum roller to expel air bubbles, working in all directions (press down awkward corners with your fingers). Push down all edges with a stair tool so that they butt up neatly against the wall.

Step 5
Roll the flooring back down onto the floor, pressing it firmly onto the adhesive and smoothing it into place as you unroll. Stretch with a knee kicker from the center toward the walls to remove any looseness. Leave the floor for 20 minutes while the adhesive begins to set. Then roll back the flooring from the other end of the room until you reach the beginning of the glued section, and repeat the process. Deal with small seamed areas separately, taking extra care to press the edges of seams firmly into the adhesive.

Step 7
Fit the flooring at the doorway into your chosen transition molding (page 125). Leave the adhesive to dry overnight, then sweep and vacuum the room to remove all trimmings.

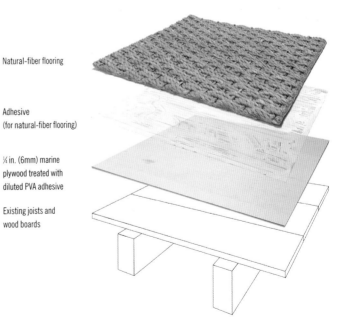

Natural-fiber flooring

Adhesive (for natural-fiber flooring)

Leveling compound

Concrete subfloor

Laying on a wood subfloor

Natural-fiber flooring

Adhesive (for natural-fiber flooring)

¼ in. (6mm) marine plywood treated with diluted PVA adhesive

Existing joists and wood boards

LEVEL OF DIFFICULTY
●●●●○

This method is complicated by the need to install padding and tackless strips.

Tool box

1. HAMMER
2. DRILL WITH MASONRY BIT (FOR A CONCRETE SUBFLOOR)
3. METAL SNIPS
4. UTILITY KNIFE AND EXTRA BLADES
5. DUCT TAPE
6. PAINT ROLLER
7. STAPLE GUN (FOR A WOOD SUBFLOOR)
8. STRAIGHTEDGE
9. PAINTER'S TAPE
10. KNEE KICKER
11. STAIR TOOL
12. LINOLEUM ROLLER

Materials

13. NATURAL-FIBER FLOORING
14. TACKLESS STRIPS
15. CARPET BAR/ THRESHOLD/Z-BAR BINDING STRIP
16. ADHESIVE (FOR PADDING AND NATURAL-FIBER FLOORING)
17. PADDING

INSTALLING A NATURAL-FIBER FLOOR WITH PADDING

Preparing the roll

As for *Installing a natural-fiber floor without padding* (☞ page 136). You can use a handheld metal detector to establish the position of any pipes before nailing tackless strips to the subfloor. Make sure you buy the correct "blind" tackless strips, without any pins (ask your supplier for advice).

Step 1

Nail down the appropriate tackless strips for your floor (☞ page 125) along the edges of the room, using a hammer on wood subfloors and a drill with a masonry bit on concrete subfloors. Position the strips at just under the thickness of the flooring away from the wall, with the manufacturer's name (printed on the surface of the strips) facing you so that you can read it. Cut the strips to fit around corners and obstacles with metal snips or a hacksaw.

Step 2

Nail or screw down a carpet bar, threshold, Z-bar binding strip or tackless strip in the doorway, depending on your chosen method of flooring transition (☞ page 125).

Step 3

Unroll the padding to cover the floor, cutting to size with a utility knife. The edges should butt up against each other and against (but not on top of) the tackless strips, without any overlapping. Seal seams with duct tape. Then roll back half the padding, and spread a thin layer of adhesive using a paint roller. Replace the padding, and repeat for the other half. Alternatively, secure with a staple gun, with staples every inch (2.5cm) around the edges and at 6 in. (15cm) intervals across the rest of the room.

Step 4

If you have used adhesive to secure the padding, leave to dry for an hour (try pulling up one corner to test if the padding is properly stuck down). Then roll out the flooring to cover the room, starting from the longest, straightest wall.

Step 5

Use a sharp utility knife and a straightedge to trim the edges to fit, cutting into recesses and doorways and around pipes. Change blades frequently. Make small slits in each of the corners to allow the flooring to lie flat (avoid cutting into the floor area).

Step 6

If you need to join sections of flooring, leave them overlapping by about 3 in. (7.5cm), secured with painter's tape, until all the cutting has been done and the covering fits perfectly around the edges. Then cut through both pieces simultaneously, using the utility knife and straightedge, to create seam edges that match exactly. (Do not try to join pieces selvage to selvage as they will not be straight enough.)

Step 7

Roll back the covering at the end of the room furthest from the exit, until about half the floor is exposed. Pour a little adhesive onto the padding and spread with a notched trowel or paint roller until the exposed section is thinly covered, including the tackless strips.

Step 8
Roll the flooring back down onto the floor, pressing it firmly onto the adhesive and smoothing it into place as you unroll. Stretch with the knee kicker, working from the center of the room toward the wall to remove any looseness. Then tuck in the edges behind the tackless strips, using a stair tool.

Step 10
When the entire floor is laid, use the knee kicker to remove any remaining looseness. Then use a linoleum roller to expel air bubbles, working in all directions (press down awkward corners with your fingers).

Step 9
Roll back the flooring from the other end of the room until you reach the beginning of the glued section, and repeat the process as above. Deal with small seamed areas separately, taking care to press the edges of seams firmly into the adhesive. If you have trimmed the door and door casing to accommodate the new floor level, use the stair tool to push the flooring neatly under the door casing.

Step 11
Fit the flooring at the doorway into your chosen transition bar (☛ page 125), stretching out any slackness with the knee kicker. Leave the adhesive to dry overnight, then vacuum and sweep the room to remove all trimmings.

THE FLOORING LAYERS

Laying on a concrete subfloor

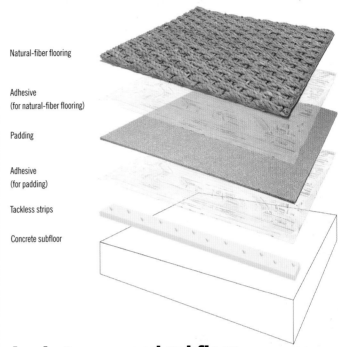

Natural-fiber flooring

Adhesive
(for natural-fiber flooring)

Padding

Adhesive
(for padding)

Tackless strips

Concrete subfloor

Laying on a wood subfloor

Natural-fiber flooring

Adhesive
(for natural-fiber flooring)

Padding

Adhesive
(for padding)

Tackless strips

Existing joists and
wood boards

GLOSSARY

ACCLIMATIZATION A period of time before installation during which wood-based flooring products adjust to the temperature and humidity of the site.

ACOUSTIC PANEL An underlayment, comprising fiberboard and compressed foam, that provides a rigid surface as well as thermal and sound insulation.

BASKETWEAVE A pattern in which rectangular tiles or bricks are laid in small groups, alternately horizontally and vertically, to create a checkered woven effect.

BROADLOOM Carpet supplied in a roll, as opposed to carpet tiles.

CAULKING Inserting caulking between the tiles and the walls and base of fixtures in order to waterproof the edges of a floor.

CEMENT BACKERBOARD A thin sheet of concrete and fiberglass mesh that may be used to provide a particularly rigid base for hard tiles.

CEMENT SCREED A thin layer of cement applied to a concrete floor in order to level it.

CERAMIC Manufactured "stone" made of refined clay fired at high temperatures.

CHECKERBOARD A pattern in which square tiles of two contrasting colors alternate.

CLAY Manufactured "stone" made of unrefined clay fired at high temperatures.

"CLICK" SYSTEMS Various installation systems whereby the tongues and grooves on the sides of laminated boards are slotted together without gluing. Also found on some engineered wood boards.

ENGINEERED WOOD BOARD A manufactured wood board composed of a thin hardwood layer attached to a softwood base. Usually supplied prefinished and with tongues and grooves.

EXPANSION GAP A ½ in. (1.25cm) gap left at the edges of a room to allow for the natural expansion and contraction of wood or laminate boards.

FLATWEAVE Woven carpet without a pile.

FLOATING FLOOR An engineered wood or laminate floor that is held down by its own weight and does not need to be glued or nailed to the subfloor.

GLAZING Applying a decorative and waterproof coating to a manufactured "stone" tile.

GROUTING Holding tiles in place and waterproofing the floor by inserting grout into the gaps between the tiles and around the edges of the room.

GROUTING GAP A space left between tiles, and at the edges of the floor, to allow grout to be inserted.

HERRINGBONE A pattern in which rectangular tiles or bricks are laid in rows that slope in opposite directions, creating a fish-bone effect.

HOT-GLUE SEAMING TAPE Used to bind carpet seams. The adhesive on the tape is heated and the carpet edges are pushed down onto the tape.

LAMINATE A simulated floor effect, often of wood, attached to high-density fiberboard (HDF).

LEVELING COMPOUND A mix of liquid latex and latex powder that is used to level a concrete subfloor.

LINOLEUM A biodegradable flooring made from linseed oil, wood and cork flour, pine resin, ground limestone and jute.

MARINE PLYWOOD Waterproof plywood used in ship-building. This is the recommended material for leveling a wood subfloor, but exterior-grade plywood may be used instead if properly treated with diluted PVA adhesive.

NON-WOVEN Carpet made by gluing synthetic fibers to a backing.

PARQUET Small, thick wood blocks laid individually to create a pattern such as herringbone.

PAVER A brick produced in varying thicknesses for flooring purposes.

PERIMETER-BOND INSTALLATION Sheet flooring glued around the edges and at the seams only.

PICKLING A traditional finish that bleaches wood and highlights the grain.

PILE The carpet fiber visible above the backing. Varies in length and thickness, and may be cut, left looped or cut and looped.

PREFINISHED A wood or laminate board supplied by the manufacturer with a protective surface already in place. Needs no further finishing.

PVA ADHESIVE White glue.

RADIANT HEATING Underfloor heating supplied in the form of a network of hot-water pipes or heated wire-mesh matting.

RUNNING BOND A pattern in which rectangular tiles or bricks are orientated in the same direction with staggered joints.

SNAPPING A CHALK LINE Securing and extending a chalked string and then snapping it onto the floor to mark a straight line.

SUBFLOOR The floor underneath the finished floor covering. Usually concrete or wood joists and floorboards, plus any underlayments used.

TACKLESS STRIPS Lengths of wood with pins used to secure soft-floor coverings at the edges of the room. "Blind" tackless strips do not have pins.

TERRA-COTTA Manufactured "stone" made of clay fired at lower temperatures than ceramic or clay tiles.

TERRAZZO Stone chips (usually marble or granite) laid in concrete or resin. Also known as Venetian mosaic.

TESSERAE Small colored pieces used in mosaic. Usually sold attached to a backing in the form of a mosaic tile.

TONGUES AND GROOVES Protuberances and slits machined onto the side of wood and laminate boards to allow the boards to fit together neatly.

TRANSITION MOLDING A wood, plastic or metal strip that provides a transition between different floors.

TUFTED Carpet manufactured by feeding yarn through a polypropylene backing sheet.

UNDERLAYMENT Anything that is installed under the final floor covering, such as waterproofing, marine plywood or foam.

WATERPROOFING A polyethylene sheet (suitable for waterproofing) or liquid damp-proof membrane applied as an underlayment to protect a floor from rising moisture.

WELDING ROD Thin strips of linoleum melted into linoleum seams to fuse them.

WOVEN Carpet produced on a loom, with an interlocking warp and weft.

INDEX

CREDITS

The author and publishers would like to thank **Richard Mills** for demonstrating the step-by-step floor-laying techniques photographed throughout this book. Thanks also to **Brian Tanner** for set building and the brick-laying demonstration. Many thanks also to the following contributors of materials and equipment for photography:

Preparing the site: F. Ball and Co. (www.f-ball.co.uk)

Laying a ceramic and clay floor: Reed Harris (www.reedharris.co.uk); www.carvallgroup.com; H & R Johnson Tiles (www.johnson-tiles.com)

Laying a terra-cotta floor: Fired Earth (www.firedearth.co.uk)

Laying a mosaic floor: Ceramic Prints (01484 400083)

Laying a slate floor: Burlington Stone (www.burlingtonstone.co.uk)

Laying a limestone and sandstone floor: Stonell (www.stonell.com)

Laying a brick floor: Dennis Ruabon (www.dennisruabon.co.uk);

Laying a vinyl floor: Karndean (www.karndean.com); Forbo-Nairn (www.nairn-cushionflor.co.uk)

Laying a cork floor: Amorim (www.amorim.com)

Laying a linoleum floor: Forbo-Nairn (www.nairn-cushionflor.co.uk)

Laying a rubber floor: Altro (www.altro.co.uk)

Laying a leather floor: Harcourt (www.harcourt.uk.com)

Laying a floating wood floor: Kahrs (www.kahrs.com)

Laying a glued solid-wood floor and Laying a nailed solid-wood floor: Atkinson & Kirby (www.akirby.co.uk)

Finishing a wood floor: Ronseal (www.ronseal.co.uk)

Laying a laminated floor: BHK (www.bhkuniclic.com)

Laying a carpeted floor: Victoria Carpets (01562 823400); Balta (www.balta.be); Duralay (www.duralay.co.uk); Burmatex (www.burmatex.co.uk)

Laying a natural-fiber floor: The Alternative Flooring Company (www.alternative-flooring.co.uk)

CREDITS CONTINUED

Quarto would like to thank and acknowledge the following for supplying pictures to be reproduced in this book:

(Key: l left, r right, c center, t top, b bottom)

Front cover, 13r (3rd from top), 73, 86, 87 • Forbo-Nairn Ltd
   www.forbo-linoleum.co.uk www.marmoleum.co.uk
2, 127tl • Victoria Carpets Pty Ltd www.victoria-carpets.com.au
4, 105bl • Bruce Hardwood Floors www.brucehardwoodfloors.com
6b, 17, 19bl, 26br, 101 (tapping block + bar), 124l (all 5) •
   The Floorwise Group www.floorwise.co.uk
7, 76r (all 3), 77l, 77tr, 77br • Karndean International Ltd www.karndean.co.uk
13l (3rd from top), 29r, 30br • Ironrock Capital, Inc www.ironrockcapital.com
   www.metroceramics.com
13l (4th from top), 35r (all 3), 42bl • Country Floors www.countryfloors.com
13l (7th from top), 127bl, 129tr • The Tintawn Weaving Company
   www.tintawncarpets.com
13l (8th from top), 134l (all 4), 134c (1st, 3rd + 4th from top), 135l •
   Crucial Trading www.crucial-trading.com www.naturalflooring.net
13c (1st from top, 3rd from top), 47, 48, 53r, 54tl, 54bl, 54tr, 64l (all 4), 65l,
   65c • Stonell www.stonell.co.uk
13c (4th from top), 66, 67l • Liquid Plastics Limited www.liquidplastics.co.uk
13c (5th from top), 68l (all 5), 69l • Carina Works, Inc www.carinaworks.com
13 (wood), 99, 102, 103, 104bl, 104r, 105tl, 110bl • Kahrs Ltd
   www.kahrs.co.uk
13r (2nd from top), 82r • Dodge-Regupol Incorporated www.regupol.com
13r (4th from top), 90 • Dalsouple www.dalsouple.com
21r • Colormaker Floors Ltd www.colormakerfloors.com
23, 59r • Massimo Listri / CORBIS
58l • Conde Nast Archive / CORBIS
28l (all 3), 30tr • Original Style Limited www.originalstyle.com
28b, 30bl, 40r, 42br • Trikeenan Tileworks Inc www.trikeenan.com
28br, 34r, 35c (room setting), 41r, 54br • Ann Sacks www.annsacks.com
28tr (both) • H&R Johnson Tiles Ltd www.johnson-tiles.com
29l, 34l, 40l (both), 40c, 42t, 52br, 53l, 64r • Paris Ceramics
   www.parisceramics.com
30tl • Daltile www.daltile.com
35l • Aldershaw Handmade Tiles Ltd www.aldershaw.co.uk
41l • Mosaik Pierre Mesguich www.mosaik-mesguich.com
46l (all 6), 52tl (all 4) • Naturestone Ltd www.stone.co.uk
46c, 46r (both) • Slate World Ltd www.slateworld.com
52bl, 52tr • Stone Source www.stonesource.com
58-59c • James Morris / Landmark Trust www.landmarktrust.co.uk
   Photograph taken at Wilmington Priory. The Landmark Trust, a building
   preservation charity, has restored the building. Wilmington Priory is available
   for holidays +44(0) 1628 825 925
66 • Lasar Contracts Ltd www.lasarcontracts.ltd.uk
68r, 71r • Ken Hayden / RED COVER
70 • Live Tile www.livetile.com
71l • Ed Reeve / RED COVER
76tl • The Amtico Company www.amtico.com

76bl • Cushionflor by Nairn www.forbo-flooring.co.uk
77c • Polyflor Ltd www.polyflor.com
91 • Christopher Everard / Dalsouple
94l (both), 94c (both), 95r • Crest Leather www.crestleather.com
94r (both), 95tl • Edelman Limited www.edelmanleather.com
95bl • Leather Co. +44 (0)1903 200005, +44 (0)1403 261000
104t, 105r • Junckers www.junckers.com
118l (all 8), 119l • Armstrong World Industries www.armstrong.com
118r (both), 119r • Richard Burbidge Limited www.richardburbidge.com
123, 126l (all 8), 127r, 128r, 129tl, 129br • Brinton Wade
   www.brintonwade.com
126r, 128l • Axminster Carpets Ltd www.axminster-carpets.co.uk
129bl • InterfaceFLOR www.interfaceflor.com
134c (2nd from top), 134r, 135r • The Alternative Flooring Company Ltd
   www.alternativeflooring.com

All other photographs and illustrations are the copyright of Quarto Publishing plc. While every effort has been made to credit contributors, Quarto would like to apologize should there have been any omissions or errors.

Conceived, designed and produced by
Quarto Publishing plc
The Old Brewery
6 Blundell Street
London N7 9BH

Project Editor: Fiona Robertson
Senior Art Editor: Sally Bond
Text Editors: Nick Gibbs, Ian Kearey
Designer: James Lawrence
Photographer: Paul Forrester, Colin Bowling
Illustrators: Sally Bond, James Lawrence
Proofreader: Sally MacEachern
Indexer: Pamela Ellis

Art Director: Moira Clinch
Publisher: Piers Spence